The Disciple Maker

by

Fernando Cabrera, Ed.D, LMHC.
Senior Pastor
New Life Outreach International Church
Bronx, New York

CONTENTS

Chapter One: The Proof is in the Fruit

"The Calling" Entails Taking God Seriously

God has called every believer to His service. He has a defined and prepared path established for every person called into the fold. We are called before conception and once realized, this calling will change and enhance the wellbeing and lives of all believers. Be that as it may, a burning question still remains... why is it that *most* Christians fail to take God seriously?

The answer is simple. The reason why many people do not take God seriously is because they don't fear the LORD. Today, many people worship a God whom they don't respect; many sing to a God whom they do not honor; and many pray to a God whom they don't obey. Essentially, they ignore the divine and complete calling upon their lives. They have lost all reverence for the Lord. The ultimate reason why most people fail to take God seriously is because *they do not understand or recognize the <u>greatness</u> of God.*

Many people today have created God in their own image; they have distorted, manipulated and re-shaped God in order to see Him in the likeness of their own misconceptions. How often do you hear people say, "God will understand why I'm not fully devoted to what he's telling me to do... After all, he is a *loving* God"? People who speak this way have created their own god, for they fail to acknowledge that, above all, it is He that is infinite and Almighty. Today, many people have created a God of convenience; they go to him only when they need him to make their lives easier and more comfortable.

When we don't take God seriously, we become careless. This is the indictment found in the book of Malachi; these individuals offered careless worship in dedication to the LORD. When we don't take God seriously we become careless about our devotion to the calling of God in our lives. And it is this carelessness that can cause us to take God for granted.

3

So, the question really is, what is truly required to take God seriously? First, we must understand that God is infinitely great. He is the God of "no limits". He is boundless in his power and greatness. Once you come to the revelation of how immeasurably great God is, you'll automatically recognize how supremely valuable He is to you. This is why Jesus said that a man will sell all he has to gain the "pearl of great price" (Matthew 13:46). You will come to the realization that everything else in life is insignificant when compared to the supreme value of God's infinite glory as you allow God to shine upon your heart (II Corinthians 4:4). You will learn to recognize that God is incomparable to the temporal limitedness of all things on Earth. Who on Earth would settle for a relatively insignificant rock or stone when they can have a flawless diamond? Which would you chase after if given the opportunity? The same is true when it comes to Jesus Christ, our Lord.

When you comprehend the supreme value of His infinite greatness, you will respond to your calling with all of your heart, mind, spirit, and strength. Once you recognize how supremely valuable Jesus is, you will subsequently surrender to His will. You will want to take God seriously and surrender your will to His own. When you finally experience this spiritual awakening you become a yielded vessel. If you have not received this revelation, ask God, right now, to reveal His infinite and glorious greatness to you. Ask Him to open your understanding and heart to the vastness of His power and presence. Today, His greatness compels you to a higher calling, which is worth your whole life. It is the only thing that warrants the giving of your time, treasures, and talents. And it is through His loving grace that He grants you the opportunity to serve His greatness. It is through the blood of Jesus that you are given the awesome privilege to serve His majesty, regardless of what kind of a past you have.

"The Calling" is an Appetite

Jesus' goal in life was to *please the Father*. And, Jesus' aim was to focus all of His strength, mind, spirit, and body into gratifying

4

the Father. In fact, He lived with one holy passion – to do the will of the Father. But what was the will of the Father? What was this calling upon His life, which in turn, also exemplifies the same calling we have upon our own lives?

In John 4:34, Jesus unveils the will of the Father when He said, "My food is to do the will of Him who sent Me and to accomplish his work." What was the work he was called to do? He said, "Lift up your eyes and look on the fields, they are white for harvest" (v.35) and then the scriptures go on to state in the next verse, "From that city many of the Samaritans believe in Him…" (Where is this?) From this passage of Scripture, we learn that *the work is the harvest of souls.* All of the work Jesus performed while He was here on Earth was directly related to this harvest. You will never find in the Bible Jesus doing anything in contrast to the will of the Father; Jesus persistently and consistently sought to reach the lost.

Conviction is an inner appetite. When you are hungry you are *convinced* that you need food. A hungry man becomes a person focused on satisfying a need. Likewise, a starving man is also a person who ultimately loves, craves and needs the satisfaction of that hunger. Similarly, conviction, like hunger, becomes a deeply rooted and essential element of a human being. A conviction is a personally held belief. And just like appetites and hunger, it is something you can't live without and demands your immediate focus and attention. Jesus' appetite, focus and convictions were to please the Father at all cost, by seeking and saving the lost. When you have true conviction, you will attain the vision of Jesus.

Many Christians fail to walk like Jesus did because they don't really believe that reaching the lost at any cost is one of the things that pleases God the most. When you have the conviction of Christ, you will develop a vision for the lost. And once you have this vision, it will create a passion in your heart. And, once you have this passion, you will be eager to do the work of God because you will do what you believe. If you are not carrying out the work of God, then you don't believe in it. You are only applying the parts of the Bible you have decided are credible and worth your belief! Take the time to break these arguments in your heart; remember, what pleases your heavenly Father is to rescue the multitude of souls who need Jesus Christ as their Lord and Savior. When you allow this conviction to be ingrained into your heart, you will love to continue the work of the Lord and you will do it without hesitation. Develop a love for God's vision for souls, because you will not do the work unless you love it. If you truly love God's vision, then you will work the vision. Again, you will not be completely faithful to the work of Jesus unless you have a love for the lost. And if you love, you will do it because you have the conviction of Jesus that pleases the Father; it is the pleasure of the Father that should cause all to rejoice!

Why don't people in church rejoice for what pleases the heart of God? Jesus provides an explanation for this occurrence in Luke 15:4-32. Here, Jesus explains what the Pharisaic and religious spirit is like. We realize that it is a Pharisaic heart that does not rejoice as God rejoices when souls come to Jesus; they are just like the brother of the prodigal son. But contrastingly, in Luke 16:3-7, we find the shepherd rejoicing when he sought and found the lost sheep. Then, in the next passage we find the widow rejoicing when she sought and found the lost coin. And back in chapter 15:11-32, we find the Father rejoicing when his lost son came back home. The joy of heaven is to win souls (Luke 15:7). Jesus' joy was for lost souls and the discipling of each (John 4:1). This is also highlighted in I John 2:4-6. John the Beloved said, "The one who says, 'I have come to know Him', and does not keep his commandments, is a liar, and the truth is not in him... the one who says he abides in him ought himself to walk in the same manner as he walked." How did Jesus walk? What did Jesus do? What did Jesus accomplish? He went about winning souls and making disciples. And if the truth is working in you, you should be working for harvest of souls as well.

Hungry anyone?

We find in John 4:34 that the thing that energized Jesus the most was soul winning. Doing God's work is what motivated and strengthened the Lord Jesus Christ (v. 34). Food invigorates and revives the body. For Jesus, making disciples was the "food" that invigorated and revived His spirit. Why? It is because the delight of Jesus was to do the will of the Father. And the will of the Father was to win and disciple souls. What's your food in life?

In this same chapter, the disciples came back from shopping and seemed more interested in having lunch than in reaching the broken Samaritan (v. 27, 31). Sometimes we are more interested in meeting our own needs than taking advantage of the opportunities God has given us. What opportunities has God been presenting to you for winning souls? Which of your personal dreams and ambitions are stopping you from reaching your friends and family for Christ?

"The Calling" is a Vision

Jesus commanded the disciples in John 4:35 to "look." He asked the disciples to "lift up" their "eyes" and see. See what? He wanted the disciples to focus their attention in reaching *people*. Disciples of Jesus should focus on the goal of reaching their family, friends, neighbors, and even enemies to be saved and walk like Christ. It would be arrogant for any man to say "this is the way" if the Scriptures shows Jesus doing it in a different way. Jesus' strategy was to win, consolidate, disciple, and send. He reached them, kept them, taught them, and sent them to provide the same message and tactics they had received.

And why was this done?

God wanted to establish a family, that is, the family of God. From the very beginning, God called man and woman to be fruitful and multiply. The very first command to Adam and Eve was to be "fruitful and multiply" (Genesis 1:28). Have you ever noticed that everything living multiplies? If you are not growing and multiplying then you are dying. This is why some Christians often feel empty inside. The emptiness stems from the absence of their multiplicative purpose in Christ. It is within our spiritual DNA to produce fruit and multiply. God called you to be a *father and/or mother of multitudes* (Genesis 17:4). It makes no sense to grow spiritually or study the Bible without having someone else to pass it on unto! *You will never have success without a successor*; God intended for the church to experience expansion through multiplication.

The early church was a church that began to grow through addition. In Acts 2:41 and 2:47, the apostle Luke in writing the Book of Acts, uses the Greek work *prostithemi*, which means "to add one thing to another". They were winning souls and adding to the church daily. We also find that by the time of Acts 4:4, the church had added about 25,000 members. These are good numbers even by today's standards; many church officials would love to have such a vast congregation. Even so we find yet another shift in the method employed by the apostles. In Acts 6, the church began add and multiply. We find stunning growth using the model of multiplication. The Greek word used now changes to *plethuno*, which means "to cause to increase" hence, "to multiply" (Acts 6:1,7; 9:31; 12:24). They understood that if they were going to reach their generation for God, they would need to experience exponential growth through multiplication.

Let's explore the concept of multiplication further. Suppose two Christians decided to win their world for Jesus. One would set a goal to win 1,000 people a day and the other would set a goal to multiply by twelve people every year. Winning 1,000 people for Christ a day would be fantastic feat. But do you know that in order for that believer to win the entire world population for Christ it would take him 10,000 years? This is not even accounting for the countless of billions of people who would be born in those 10,000 years. But if the other Christian were just to multiply by twelve every year, he would reach the entire population of the world in just nine generations. (See the Illustration Below)

The Tower of Multiplication

12 - First Year

144- Second Year

1728- Third Year

20,000- Fourth Year

240,000- Fifth Year

2,880,000- Sixth Year

34,560,000- Seventh Year

414,720,000- Eighth Year

4,976,640,000- Ninth Year

59,719,680,000- Tenth Year

(Exceeding Earth's population by almost 54 billion people)

*Please Note: The population of the entire world is only about 6.5 billon people; if applied, the entire world be reached well before the end of the Tenth Year!

The difference is both obvious and incredible! Addition can never catch up with multiplication.   The New Testament church understood this principle. The great thing is that the Lord used ordinary people to accomplish extraordinary results. And He used people just like you and I.

Some people disqualify themselves by thinking that they need to be perfect in order to be a disciple maker or leader. God is looking for those who are hungry and thirsty to be touched and used of the Lord.   In Mark 3:14, it states, "[Jesus] appointed twelve, designating them apostles, that they might be with him and that he might send them out to preach."   It's apparent that Jesus understood the power of multiplication. I like the way D. L. Moody said it, "I'd rather put 10 people to work than do the work of 10 people."

The apostle Paul understood this principle of multiplication as well. In II Timothy 2:2, Paul provides a strategy of multiplication to his disciple Timothy. He tells Timothy, to pass on to "faithful men" what he taught them. Notice what he did *not* say? He did not use the singular noun "man", but its plural form, "men." Timothy, Paul's disciple, was instructed to pass the Gospel on to multiple people who were then to pass it on to others. This principle of multiplication brought multitudes to the feet of Jesus; thousands were healed and cleansed of their sins; countless people received a passion for our Savior. By reading the word, we know that Jesus came for the lost and sent His disciples for the lost as well. In turn, these men sent forth others to do the same... what would the world have looked like if these men had disobeyed the Father? Not a pretty picture, is it?

One of these days, you may actually come across someone who opposes the principle of multiplication. Interestingly enough, these same individuals ask the LORD to multiply their finances or other opportunities! It's intriguing to see that here, when needed, people are willing to believe in the principle of multiplication. How can a dollar be worth more than a soul? Are we willing to ask God for personal blessings but not for the increase of His kingdom through lost souls? Do we actually believe that God is willing to increase our financial situations and personal lives but not the body of Christ?

Multiplication takes place through "parenting" in the natural world, and, the same should be expected in the spiritual world as well. When we refer to parenting, we are referring to a healthy approach of mentoring. Even the world recognizes the importance of mentoring. Did you know that 50% of the head coaches in the NFL during the year 1998 can be traced back to two outstanding former pro football leaders – Bill Walsh and Tom Landry?

Similarly, the healthy development of children is the responsibility of fathers and mothers; the same is true in the kingdom.

Today, people don't just want to believe, they want to belong; people want to be connected. They want someone to impart wisdom and guidance upon their lives. You may say, "I am too busy to get involve in other people's lives!" If you are too busy to make disciples, then you are too busy for God.

If Jesus was here physically on Earth, how would He spend His time and where would He go? We find in the gospels that Jesus loved to spend and invest His time with people. But the interesting aspect about this is where Jesus invested His time. We find that Jesus made 132 contacts with different people throughout the gospels. Six times we find him in the temple. Four times we find him in the synagogue. But, the other 122 times, Jesus can be found in the neighborhoods where ordinary people lived and mingled. Some may say that Jesus spent most of His time in the neighborhood and with the people. His purpose was focused on people. The pressures He went through were for the benefit of the people. His passion was centered on the people. His prayers were for the people. His power was released upon the people and Jesus was fired up about having a *harvest of people*.

Are you a mule or sheep?

A mule is an interesting animal; it is one of the few animals that cannot breed. Why? Mules are the consequence of crossbreeding! Both a male donkey and a female horse are needed to create this distinctive creature. Mules are able to work extremely hard and carry tremendous loads for their owners, making them valuable assets; however, they cannot produce offspring. When comparing sheep and mules, the dissimilarities are virtually undeniable; mules, though useful, can never produce another generation! If a farmer desires more mules for their flock, they must go back to a mare and a jack (donkey stallion) in order to increase their fold. No matter how many mules are retained, the owners will never see the physical reproduction of any prized mules. On the other hand,

11

sheep reproduce proficiently and naturally. This occurrence can involve little to no effort on the part of the farmer. Left to themselves, sheep will breed with or without human intervention; reproduction takes places at a steady rate during mating season.

Many people in churches are just like mules; although ready and willing to help, they never reproduce. These individuals can be diligent and earnest in church, but they do not produce a new generation of disciples for the Lord.

We have people today who work very hard in ministry, but are not multiplying. They pray hard, study hard, minister hard, but die hard! I can relate to these churchgoers because I used to be one of them. These members are faithful, but not fruitful. They are also faithful but frustrated. Statistics shows that only 10% of Christians have ever told somebody else about Jesus and only 1% have ever discipled a person for Christ. Pastor Jack Hanes said, "Jesus' last command should be our first priority."

God expects us to be both faithful and fruitful. Fruitfulness is a major theme of the New Testament. We are called by Jesus to bear fruit. He said, "You did not choose me, but I chose you and appointed you to go and bear fruit – fruit that will last" (John 15:16). God wants to see lasting fruit come from our ministry. Being fruitful is a way we glorify God: "This is to my Father's glory, that you bear much fruit, showing yourselves to be my disciples" (John 15:8). An unfruitful ministry does not bring glory to God, but a fruitful ministry is the proof that we are Christ's disciples. Being fruitful pleases God: "We pray this in order that you may live a life worthy of the Lord and may please him in every way, bearing fruit in every good work" (Col. 1:10). Did you know that Jesus reserved his severest judgment for an unfruitful fig tree? He cursed it because it didn't bear fruit. "Seeing a fig tree by the road, he went up to it but found nothing on it except leaves. Then he said to it, 'May you never bear fruit again!' Immediately the tree withered" (Matt. 21:19). Jesus did not do this to show off but to make a point: He expects fruitfulness! The nation of Israel lost its privilege because of unfruitfulness. When speaking regarding Israel, Jesus said, "Therefore I tell you that the kingdom of God will be taken away from you and given to a people who will produce its fruit" (Matt. 21:43).

One of the main fruits of a believer is to *win* another person to Christ. Paul said he wanted to preach in Rome "in order that I might obtain some fruit among you also, even as among the rest of the Gentiles" (Romans 1:13). Notice that Paul the apostle referred to the first converts in Achaia as the "first fruit of Achaia" (I Cor. 16:15). Colossians 1:6 says, "All over the world this gospel is bearing fruit and growing, just as it has been doing among you since the day you heard it."

God also wants you to be successful. Success is to fulfill the Great Commission (Matthew 28:28-30). The opposite of success is not failure, but faithlessness. Any church member, ministry leader or believer that is not obeying the Great Commission is failing to fulfill their purpose, no matter what else they do. Success is bearing as much fruit as possible with your gifts, opportunities, and potential. We are taught in the parable of the talents (Matthew 25:14-30) that those who were considered faithful were fruitful. Christ doesn't expect us to produce more than we can, but He does expect us to produce all that we can through *His* power, which is working within us. That is a lot more than most of us think physically or spiritually possible.

Decide today to become the best multiplier and to reproduce Christ in others. God has called us to multiply. Out of you can come twelve strengthened believers, of those twelve, each can do the same, creating 144 strengthened believers, and those 144 can create 1,728 strengthened believers, and so on. The apostle Paul said, "For if I preach the Gospel, I have nothing to boast of, for necessity is laid upon me; yes, woe is me if I do not preach the Gospel!" (1 Corinthians 9:16) God opened Paul's spiritual eyes and he could clearly see the tragedy of remaining silent. This revelation gave him responsibility and motivated his commitment to it. Paul said, "and his grace toward me was not in vain, but I labored more abundantly than they all, yet not I, but the grace of God which was with me" (1 Corinthians 15:10).

The entire world is lost and God has entrusted to you and every disciple of Jesus the responsibility of spreading the Gospel, which can lead to the salvation of souls. Thank God that the vision that the Lord has given us has the complete package, because you will not only win them, but God gives you the wisdom to consolidate them, disciple them, and send them to do the same.

In a two-year study done by renowned researcher George Barna, it was found that most born again Christians don't see their lives' goal as being a committed disciple of Jesus or of making disciples. Only one out of every ten Christians ever leads someone to the Lord. And far less have ever made a disciple. He found that "... Christians spend seven times as much time on entertainment as they do on spiritual activities…and that desiring to have a close, personal relationship with God ranks just sixth among the 21 life goals tested, trailing such desires as 'living a comfortable lifestyle.'" *Today, convenience has taken over the Great Commission in many churches.*

The Calling is Personal

Jesus specifically called you out when He said in verse 35 "I say to YOU." (verse 35 of what?) The calling of God is a personal call to please the Father by working the harvest of souls. It is a personal call to those who have come to the revelation that Jesus is infinitely glorious and therefore supremely valuable. Every personal call from God comes with a call to faithful obedience.

In Luke 6:46, Jesus emphatically asked us, "Why do you call Me, 'Lord, Lord' and do not do what I say?" Do you understand what Jesus is saying here? In other words, Jesus is saying that if you accepted Him as infinitely great and most valuable, how is it that your actions do not match what you say? Since it is a personal call, we can't excuse ourselves. It is an awesome privilege to be personally called of God. God does care tremendously if you heed

14

to His call or not. The calling reveals the heart. His Word reveals the condition of our soul. *The seed reveals the condition of the soil.* Just like a seed reveals the condition of a soil, so the seed of the Word of God reveals the condition of your heart. If your heart is eager to engage in full devotion to God, it will respond with an exuberant joy at the call of God to reap souls for Jesus. But if the soil of your heart is full of self-interest, selfishness, greed, or the like, it will respond with hesitation and procrastination towards fulfilling the will of God. In Mark 4:1-20, Jesus clearly states that when the Word is spoken unto our hearts, the condition of it will be revealed. The only condition of the heart Jesus is pleased with is the type of heart that is *fertile for fruitfulness.* When you understand that you have a personal calling on your life to bear fruit and you *surrender* to it, you will experience a harvest of multiplication.

The Calling is Urgent

Jesus passionately stated in John 4:35, "Do not say, 'There are yet four months, and then comes the harvest.'" Jesus was pinpointing that the calling is urgent. It is not to be ignored or put off. The enemy of urgency is procrastination. The quickest way to kill the urgent call of God upon your life is to come to the erroneous belief that we can wait for another time or season to reap the harvest of souls. Heaven can't wait. If we don't reap the harvest it will rot. Farmers know too well that they only have a short window of opportunity to bring in the harvest. If they failed to do so in a timely fashion, they will end up fruitless.

The root of procrastination is self-justification. At the core of every instance of procrastination you will always find an excuse. The excuse may be "I am too busy now", "I will do the call of God when my children become adults", "I have more important things to do right now", "I will do it when I get married", and so on. God never accepts excuses. Why? Excuses keep us from experiencing the blessing and blessing others. You will never change as long as you live in the excuse zone. You will tolerate whatever you justify. A wise man once said, "Procrastination are the nails used to build a house of failure." (who said this? Because the grammar doesn't make any sense) You can't excuse your way into success in the things of God. My son Joshua says it well, "There are no excuses in heaven."

Jesus told us that we need to stop speaking words that kill the sense of urgency in our spirit. The question that you need to answer is, "Is it worth it?" Those who understand that people matter because they matter to God are those who will feel the urgency to win souls and make disciples. We need to come to a place where we can understand the eternal worth of a person compared to the temporal value of things here on Earth. If you place your interest on temporal things here on Earth, you will find it difficult to value what God values in heaven. God values people. God is interested in people more than anything else here on Earth. Some look for rewards here on Earth, thus becoming easily disinterested in reaching souls for God. Know that your reward is in heaven. There is a story of a missionary who came back to the Unites States after serving the Lord for 40 years in the mission field. As the plane was landing, he noticed outside hundreds of people cheering. He thought to himself, "Wow, there are hundreds of people who have come out to celebrate my homecoming." However, before he stepped out of the plane, this same crowd began to cheer at a rock star that was stepping out of the plane before him. He soon realized that these people were not there to celebrate his long years of serving God in harsh conditions, but to cheer a rock star. He soon became discouraged and asked the Lord, "How is it possible that this rock star, who is polluting the minds of young people, is celebrated, but I come home and there is not even one person to celebrate this moment?" The Lord lovingly replied back to him, "Son, the reason why there is no celebration and reward now is because you are not home yet!" There will be a day when the Lord will compensate your service to God. As a child of God, you need to understand that you cannot delay in your calling. Many are depending on it. Let a heavenly urgency build within you and thrust you into a season of fruitfulness and multiplication.

The Calling is Work

Jesus plainly stated that He was here to "accomplish the work". Many churches in America have become churches of knowing and not doing. If knowing alone was enough, why is attendance declining in 85% of churches in America while we know more theology and biblical information now than ever before? Many have become professional talkers. But Jesus is not in the business of raising biblical scholars who only know, but refuse to act. Jesus put it this way, "Why do you call me Lord and do not do what I say?" (Luke 6:46) There is an inconsistency when we just talk the talk without walking the walk. It is a contradiction to say Jesus is Lord without yielding to Him with faith-based obedience.

In Proverbs 14:23, the wisest man who ever lived said, "In all labor there is profit, but mere talk leads only to poverty." There is a poverty of ministry and service to God when we refuse to work the harvest of souls. Working the calling of God is never in vain. Jesus only considered those who do the will of God as part of the family of God. "But he answered and said to them, 'My mother and My brothers are these who hear the word of God and do it.'" (Luke 8:21) Those who have placed their faith in God will do the works of faith. Works do not save us, but a saving faith works! It moves us into action. Today's churches are full of church members, but few disciples makers. Some will say, "I am serving God my own way." But, keep in mind that God Almighty will not bless a mess, stubbornness, or private agendas. God wants us to do the work His way. Imagine you go to your job and you tell your boss, "I am no longer doing work here as instructed to me. I am going to do it my own way." It does not take a genius to know that you would soon be doing your own thing as an ex-employee of the company. The same is true in the kingdom of God. God is the King and CEO in the kingdom of heaven. He has a plan already established for us to work. All we have to do is to work it. Thank God He does not expect us to invent a strategy for doing his work. He has already provided the plan, all we have to do is put it into action. There is no substitute for work in the kingdom of God.

The Calling is to Complete what Christ Started

Jesus was not only satisfied with doing the work but finishing it. He tells us in John 4:34 that he came to "accomplish" it. This is the same Greek word found in Acts 20:24, when Paul said "But I do not consider my life of any account as dear to myself, so that I may *finish my course* and the ministry which I received from the Lord Jesus..." Many people are quick and eager to start something, but are quickly given to quitting. If there is something God can't stand it is when we quit. Why? He cannot accomplish anything through someone who quits. Jesus provided us an example through his life to finish what we have started (Hebrews 12:1-3). God has given you a mighty calling and He expects you to complete what you have started.

Jesus' Method of Making Disciples

Jesus did not leave disciple making to chance. He had a method and strategy in making disciples who were going to change the world. In the last 25 years, the church around the world has begun to rediscover these golden nuggets of truth about discipleship from the life of Jesus. Notably, Pastor Cesar Castellanos has been at the forefront of this discovery. He calls this methodology of discipleship the Ladder of Success. Basically, the Ladder of Success is a four-step process of discipleship, where we win, consolidate, disciple, and send. We will now be learning each of these steps and how to implement them effectively in order to win souls and make disciples for Jesus.

Chapter Two: Winning by Reaching

The first step on the ladder of success is to *win* souls. At New Life Outreach International we have *three evangelistic values* that serve as a driving force to win souls. We teach that God *is* interested in numbers, the church should focus on quality *and* quantity, and that evangelism is *our* responsibility. There are people in Christianity today who teach that God is not interested in numbers. That is an amazing and confusing claim, since Jesus died for every single soul on the face of the Earth. We count people because people count! We count what we value. We count money because we value it. Why then wouldn't we count people, who have a far greater value than money? Jesus said, "Go into the highways and byways that my house may be FULL" (biblical verse). (where in the Bible?) If God was not interested in numbers, He would not have asked the servant to go back to the "highways and edges" to bring in more people into his house. A church can have a healthy balance between quality and quantity. I have learned that the more quantity you have the more quality you can provide. And the more quality you have, the more quantity you can have.

In small churches, people become experts in justifying the lack of growth. I know because I was one of them! I also know that many pastors and leaders are working harder than ever. It is a frustrating thing to see little growth in the light of all the effort and work leaders devote to their congregations. But we must be careful not to correlate lack of quantity to having quality. We find in the New Testament church, leaders and disciples focused on increasing in quantity while developing quality. God wants a multiplication of disciples and he wants disciples who carefully create mature disciples. Quality and quantity are not mutually exclusive. We have been commissioned to reach as many souls as possible. For your church to grow, you must develop an unshakeable conviction that God wants your church to grow (Col. 2:19; 2 Peter 3:9). The church that doesn't want to grow and multiply is basically saying to the world, "You can go to hell." When you keep your mouth shut and you don't tell the people about Jesus and what He can do for them, you're basically saying, "You can be eternally lost forever." Pastor Rick Warren said it best when he wrote, "If I had the cure for AIDS or cancer I would be in the streets shouting it. It would be criminal to know the solution and not tell other people. But I know something even more important – how to have the purpose of life here on Earth and how to have eternal life in heaven. There's nothing more important than that. You know it too. It's our duty to pass it on. The Great Commission is not an option to be considered, but a command to be obeyed."

A Vision Fueled by Compassion

Like a father and mother, we need to develop a passion for spiritual children who need fathering and mothering. We need to develop compassion for the spiritual children God has allowed us to mentor. The fuel of the vision of multiplication is compassion. Compassion is what moves you to reach the "unwanted" people and nurture them as a father would nurture his lost child. There is no sacrifice too great when a person is full of compassion. It is less of a concept we try to define than something we do. It is more than an "I feel sorry for you" moment but something we actually *do* to meet a need. Compassion without action is a contradiction. This is why compassion will always move you to action. Compassion is fully birthed when it is manifested in reaching out to others. What is the goal of compassion? The goal of compassion is *total restoration.* The New Testament knows nothing of a Christian witnessing with compassion without the intent for conversion.

The focus of evangelizing is in *finding*. Compassion moves you to not only seek, but to find. Let me illustrate this point. When the *Titanic* was sinking, it has been estimated that most of the lifeboats were only filled to half to capacity. The lifeboats should have been filled to capacity when the Titanic was about to sink. What was even more tragic is the fact that only one of these small vessels ever came back to rescue those who were floating in the water after the Titanic sank. Eyewitnesses tell us that those in the rescue boats were more concerned about their own wellbeing and safety and that the wails of the shipwrecked only moved one boat of survivors to come back and rescue those who were freezing to death in the water. What caused the few rescuers to go back? It was the stirring heart of compassion. The tragedy of it all is that in the discussion of whether or not they should go back, they actually lost precious moments for rescue. By the time they went back to save those floating in the freezing water, they were only able to find six people alive. Hundreds of others froze to death *while* waiting for rescuers. Let's keep in mind that the church is not a luxury liner, it is a rescue ship. The question for the church to ask itself is this: are we filling our spiritual lifeboats to capacity? We find in the parables of Jesus an emphasis in not just searching but finding the lost. In the parable of the lost coin, the woman did not just search. She did not stop until she found the lost coin. In the parable of the lost sheep, the shepherd did not stop searching until found the lost sheep. In the parable of the Wedding Feast, the servant is told to go into the "highways and byways" and compel them to come in after the first time he had went out and was rejected by those who were first invited. In Ezekiel 34, we find harsh words to shepherds who substitute other activities for finding the lost and bringing them home. God is not pleased by the excuse that his servant is doing something "more spiritual" than searching for strayed sheep. Nothing is more important to God than reconciliation. If reconciliation is the main thing, then everything we do in church and outside of church must reflect the same.

Jesus' heart is for the lost sheep. In Matthew 9:35-37 and Luke 10:1-2, we find Jesus moved with compassion for the multitudes. Jesus had a tender sensitivity towards the needs of other people. He fully understood their spiritual and emotional conditions. Compassion is what drives a disciple to want to win the lost. It is compassion which cries in our hearts, "I am going to see him make it all the way through." Someone once said, "Preach to the broken heart and you will have a multitude." Compassion moves us beyond focusing just on those who seem to be acceptable members of society. If you don't have compassion, your heart will not be broken for the broken. Compassion says, "I will not stop until that person is healed." There is no sacrifice too great when a person is full of compassion. Compassion is something we *do*. It becomes less of a concept we try to define and more of something we actually do. We find again in the same chapter Jesus speaking about the need for laborers who would go after the harvest. Jesus used the story of the Good Samaritan to answer the question "Who is my neighbor?" In this story, an ordinary man sprang into action, while the religious leaders passed by a wounded man on the road to Jericho. All three of the religious men saw the hurting man, but only the Samaritan *showed* compassion. The Good Samaritan took a risk, took the first step, healed the wounds, anointed him, became a brother's keeper, and paid the price. A man or woman of God with compassion has one goal in mind for the lost: *total restoration*. The vision of Jesus is not a structure; it is a heartbeat of compassion. The fire of the vision is compassion.

We also find in Matthew 9 that Jesus called upon His disciples to pray for laborers. This is one of those few places in the New Testament where we find Jesus asking us to pray specifically for something. What kind of laborers was He asking for? He was asking for laborers that will reap the harvest. We need to ask for laborers that would "gather, bundle and bring in the harvest." The harvest was the multitudes of sheep without a shepherd. Jesus was asking us to pray for pastoral laborers. The kind of laborer he was talking about were pastoral workers who would take care of the harvest of souls. God is looking for *pastoral workers*.

The type of pastoral workers He is looking for are disciples who are not just satisfied with searching for lost souls, but finding them. Disciples who go about winning are not just content with just sharing the good news, but finding and bringing in lost souls. Are you just searching or have you decided in your heart to not stop evangelizing until you find those who are open to receive the gospel?

The Attitude of a Soul Winner (Luke 16)

A true soul winner will develop the heart of a shepherd. A shepherd will stop at nothing until he finds his lost sheep. A

22

shepherd loves his sheep. He will not settle or rest in comfort until the missing sheep comes home. In the same manner, as a disciple maker, you must learn to develop a heart of a spiritual shepherd who is moved by compassion to find the lost (Matthew 10). Stop at nothing until you find your sheep (v. 4). To "go after" implies pursuit; pursuit implies passion, passion implies purpose, and purpose implies vision. You will never possess what you are unwilling to pursue. Jesus went everywhere, including to the market (mall), boats (business), synagogue (church), and the homes of people to find the lost. He went everywhere to find the lost sheep. If Jesus went everywhere to find His twelve and the multitudes, what makes us believe that less is required of us? Jesus was reachable and reached out to bring in the down and out. God's vision propels us to find and bring back the lost sheep so they can be healed. Notice how it says that "he lays it on his shoulders" (v. 5). It implies an exhausted, beaten, and hurting sheep. Some men, women, youth, and children must be "carried" back to church from the thistles of life. The myth in churches today is that evangelists are the only ones that "go after" souls, but here in this parable we find a shepherd "going after" a sheep. In this passage, it is not speaking of following up but of winning. The cry of the heart of Jesus is for more shepherds and disciple makers who will stop at nothing until they find their lost sheep ("What man among you…" v.4). If you are not interested and passionate about seeing souls saved, you have a Pharisaic spirit who is only interested in learning but not touching lives. The joy of heaven is to win souls. Look for people who know they need help. Your rejoicing will occur when you find the lost (v.5) who will become one of the twelve disciples that you will mentor. Notice that Jesus went to those who were hurting. The great thing about reaching people is that those you reach can reach others. You are already networked with the entire world!

Be a shepherd of one, before becoming a shepherd of twelve. Learn to "go after the 'one'" (v.4). Somebody out there needs you. Don't be intimidated because you feel that you need reach great multitudes. Just seek to win one at a time. They will seldom come to you; you must go to them.

We can learn Jesus' attitude on evangelism by looking at the story of the Samaritan woman in John 4. *The first thing we find in this story is that we are to take every opportunity where God has placed you to reach a soul* (John 4:4). The Bible tells us in verse 4 that "He had to pass through Samaria". I call this divine coincidence. This is when it seems a situation is a coincidence, but really we are there for a divine appointment. You are not in your job by coincidence, your neighbor is not your neighbor by chance, your friend seated right next to you in school is not there by luck and you are not in the school you are in by happenstance. You are there because God wants you to open an opportunity to reach a soul for him. Second, *Jesus got out of His way to present her the way (v.3).* If Jesus went out of His way and went so far to reach one woman, why shouldn't we? Am I as committed to the salvation of men and woman as God is? Too often many believers expect unbelievers to come to them, while the plan of God is for us to go to them! God says, "come" to unbelievers, but "go" to the church. Third, Jesus broke *down the barriers* (v. 9). In this instance, Jesus had to break down the wall of racism. It was said at that time and place in Israel that to eat with a Samaritan was like eating with swine. They were despised because they were half Jews and half Assyrians. Too often, we tend to avoid people who are not like us. Do you see people as God sees them? There is a story of a black man who was trying to become a member of an all white church. He approached the pastor and the pastor became nervous, because his church member would have disapproved of it. He quickly came with a plan. He said to the African-American brother, "Why don't you take time to talk to Jesus and see what Jesus tells you? We don't want to rush into matters like this. Ask Jesus if He really wants you to become a member of this church." Soon after he approached the black brother, he stopped attending church and Bible studies from that time on. One day, while walking through Main Street, the pastor saw the black brother. He could not resist asking him what the Lord had said to him. So he asked, "My brother, please excuse me. But do you remember when I asked you to ask Jesus to see if he really wants you to be part of our church? What did Jesus say to you?" The black brother responded with a quick smile, "Yes, I went before the Lord and I said, 'Lord, I am trying to become a member of this church, but they are giving me a hard time.' The Lord responded back to me, 'Don't worry, I have been trying to get into that church for years and they won't let me in either.'"

This Samaritan woman had three strikes against her. She was a woman and being a woman in the first century in Jerusalem was difficult. The strictest rabbis forbade greeting woman in public. She was immoral. She was living with a man who was not her husband. And she was Samaritan, so she was racially rejected. And yet, Jesus broke through all of these manmade barriers to get a hold of her.

Next, *you must change your identity from a church attendee to a disciple maker.* We find in John 4:1-2 that Jesus saw himself as a disciple maker. God has called you to see yourself as a disciple maker as well. Often, I see people wearing a T-shirt or wristband with the letters WWJD – "What Would Jesus Do?" The answer is simply that He would make disciples. *To be a disciple of Jesus you must be committed to Him above everything else in this world, which includes serving Him as a disciple maker.*

You *will also never find Jesus apologizing for sharing the truth.* If anything, we need to apologize for not sharing the gospel sooner to friends and family. Stop apologizing and start evangelizing. Abortionists don't apologize for their stand, terrorists don't apologize for their views, and cults don't apologize for their doctrines; how much more should we not apologize for the truth? Lastly, *make people thirsty for the Lord* (v. 10, 14). Jesus did this by dealing with people's interests and needs. He focused on what people are really seeking for in life and provided the real answer to their problems.

If there was a fire in someone's house in the middle of the night, would you say, "I don't want to go over there and offend them by telling them there is a fire which is about to kill them"? Instead, you would stop everything you are doing, go over there and wake them up and get them out.

Why do we put off reaching our friends, neighbors, family, and others for Christ? It is because we have come to believe a lie. What is the lie? The lie is that people are not interested in God or spiritual matters. In fact, all research and surveys taken in the last few years show that American interest in God is going up and not down because what is occurring in our world. George Gallup found in a recent poll that 65 million Americans have no home church. But he also discovered that 34 million of those people said, "I would go to church if somebody invited me." In another Gallup survey, he discovered that teenagers in 2002 would rather talk about God and spirituality than sex, drugs, or music. Opportunities for you to share the good news are all around you. You may not realize it, but there are opportunities presented to you every day of your life. This is why the scriptures says to "be ready at all times to answer anyone who asks you to explain the hope you have in you" (1 Peter 3:15 TEV).

What we need is consistent evangelism. In Acts 5:42, we are told that "everyday" they were preaching the message of Jesus. And the best kind of evangelism is personal evangelism. Most people, who come to accept Jesus as their Lord and Savior, do so through a friend, family member, or someone they trust. We should make it a point to reach out every day to everyone we come in contact with. It is not enough to say, "They will see my life and they will get saved." They are not saved by your life, but by His death! Yes, how you live will give credibility to the gospel. But faith comes by hearing the word of God. Paul confirms this in Romans 10:14 when he says, "How will they call on Him in whom they have not believed, how will they believe in Him whom they have not heard? And how will they hear without a preacher?"

How to Pray for the Harvest

In I Timothy 2:1-3 tells us that we are to pray for all men to come to the Father through Jesus our Lord. Jesus also instructed us how to pray strategically for the church to mobilize. Based on Matthew 9:34-37, Bishop McKingly (who?) breaks down this way: (1) Thank him for the harvest ('the harvest is plentiful"), (2) ask him for the workers, for they are few ("but the workers are few"), (3) ask him to send them ("to send out workers to the harvest") (4) and finally ask the Lord "What would you have me to do?" It is not enough to pray for the harvest, but to pray for His disciples to be sent to the harvest, including ourselves.

JESUS' STRATEGY FOR WINNING SOULS

Target Potential Followers Strategically
In Mark 1, we find Jesus targeting a few men He had come to be familiar with and who had come to know Him for about a year. Peter, James and John were among the first three selected and chosen to be in Jesus' group of twelve disciples (Mark 1:16). They followed Him and became disciples. Your cell group will not grow by chance. *The fact is that no cell group or church grows without visitors.* Prospects must be strategically targeted. Jesus knew exactly whom He was going after.

How exactly did Jesus go about winning souls?
He focused on people's needs and dreams. When Jesus reached out to people He asked, "What do you want me to do for you?" (Matt.20:32; Mark 10:51; Luke 18:41). The key to opening the hearts of people is found in their "needs". Jesus tapped into the needs of the people. In America, most needs are focused on emotional and interpersonal issues. As you go out to win souls for Christ and gather people for your cell groups, you need to be conscious of the people's needs.

He focused first on friends and family who were receptive and not on those who were resistant. You can start building your cell group one by one through your circle of family and friends. Notice how none of the twelve that Jesus selected demonstrated resistance towards Him. They were all receptive. When Jesus first gave them authority to evangelize and to perform miracles, He advised them, "And if the house be worthy, let your peace come upon it:

but if it be not worthy, let your peace return to you" (Matthew 10:13). When Jesus speaks of "worthy", he is speaking of receptivity. Mike Murdock puts it this way, "Go where you are celebrated, not just tolerated." The two most receptive types of people are those who are in "transition" and/or in "tension." If you come across somebody who is going through "changes" in their lives, they are likely to be receptive to what you have to say. Of course, we want to share the gospel with everyone, but we must also be alert to those who God has placed in our path who have fertile hearts due to God's tilling of their hearts through pressure and changes in their lives. Here are some examples of people who are going through transition and/or tension:

- Second time visitors to your church
- Close friends and relatives of church members
- People going through a divorce
- Those who feel a need for a recovery program
- First time parents
- Those suffering from a terminal illness
- A couple with major marital problems
- Parents with "problem children"
- Recently unemployed persons or those with financial problems
- New residents to the community

He lived the life. Learn to not just to *do* evangelism, but become a living testimony. Everywhere you go, everyone you meet, and every time you go, there is a potential opportunity to "win" someone to Christ and bring that person into your cell group.

He invested his time in developing an inner core group. Jesus invested time with those disciples that first followed him. Notice how Jesus, after He called them, took them under his wings and showed them what ministry was all about through the demonstration of God's power and authority. He began to mentor Peter, James and John. These three became the inner core of the group of twelve. *Jesus took time to win their trust.* Jesus took these three to places and events that others did not go to. He developed this inner group so that they could serve as an example to the others. We have seen in many of our cell groups that the members of the inner core are often the ones who evangelize and recruit people for the group.

Get Involved in the Families of Future Leaders

Jesus took the time after calling Peter to be one of his twelve to go to his house to minister to his family (Mark 1:30-31). His mother in law was sick with a fever. Jesus meets her need by healing her and then she becomes part of the team by helping and serving her guests. Jesus did not want Peter to encounter any obstacle in his ministry that might arise from family distractions.

I can relate to Jesus' strategy. My twin brother was the first in my family to be saved. A high school friend led my brother to the Lord. Then they, with the love of the Lord, both focused on reaching out to me. I accepted the Lord. Then, both my brother and I led our mother to the Lord. We then reached out to our siblings. However, it didn't stop there; we ended up reaching our grandmother, uncles, aunts and cousins for the Lord.

Use Your Group Member's Family as a Home Base and Launching Pad

Jesus embarked on reaching the masses only *after* He had reached His future leaders' families. The Bible says, "And at evening, when the sun did set, they brought unto him all that were diseased, and them that were possessed with devils" (Mark 1:32). Jesus was a genius in reaching people. Paul followed the same strategy when he ministered to the jailer. He said, "Believe on the Lord Jesus Christ, and you will be saved, you and your household." Paul was targeting his household. Why? He understood that family members are already connected by trust. He knew that people trust the messenger before the trust the message.

Jesus' pattern was to reach first the individual, and through the individual reach the family, and through the family reach the community. Every person you reach opens and creates an avenue to reach others. Studies have shown that 86% of the people attracted to a church come because of a personal contact with a church member. This is an issue of trust. Families and friends have an already established this bridge of trust. It is no wonder that those who are invited and subsequently remained as members of a church viewed the invitee as a friend, rather than as a counselor or a salesman.

Lesson from the Master Fisherman

Jesus often used allegories and metaphors when He taught, and consistently used fishing as an analogy to describe outreach and evangelism. In Mark 1:17, Jesus told the disciples, "Follow Me and I will make you become fishers of men." He gives us here a clear indication that if you follow Jesus, He will make you a catcher of souls. When fishermen go to fish, the fish don't just come to the fishermen and get into the boat; you need certain instruments to achieve this task. And, just like in fishing, disciple makers need certain tools to "catch" souls for God. Let's go over the tools you need to go fishing for souls.

You Need Bait

"Bait" is the one essential article of equipment that is needed to go rod fishing. You may have the best-looking rod in the world, but if you don't have bait, you are not going to catch anything except maybe some weeds! Love is the "bait" of "one to one" evangelism. In the Gospel of John 13:35, Jesus declared it by saying, "By this shall all men know that ye are my disciples, if ye have love one to another."

Love through evangelism is best exemplified through "servant evangelism." In Pastor David Yonggi Cho's church, with a membership now nearing a million people, cell group leaders evangelize by showing acts of kindness and servanthood. If they see a need, they meet it. When the unbeliever asks, "Why are you showing me kindness?" the disciple maker shares his testimony about the love of God and the good news of the Gospel. The unbeliever is then invited to the cell group. It is difficult for someone to reject an invitation to a cell group after receiving an act of kindness. The truth is that love makes the Gospel attractive to others. Growing cells love and loving cells grow. At New Life Outreach International Church, we teach people to communicate love through a look, a word, or a touch in order to reach those who seem unreachable. Remember, many people today are not just looking for a friendly cell group, but for a friend.

The best bait you can offer is to be a blessing. Every strategy you use, whether it is by offering free coffee or chocolate in the street, raffling off a free basket full of spa products or giving out free cake by a bus or train station, must involve a blessing attitude. When people see that you are interest in becoming a blessing in their lives, they will gladly open their hearts to the Gospel message. This is the secret of winning.

Secret of Winning

The secret of winning is to be a blessing. The best strategy in the world in reaching the lost is to be a blessing to the lost. If you learn anything in this section on how to win, learn to be a blessing. The goal of a disciple maker is not to be successful but to be a blessing. Here is the good news: *God grants success to those who want to be a blessing.* Young King Solomon was blessed with riches and fame because he *first* sought to be a blessing to the people of God (I Kings 3:5-14). Joseph (Genesis chapter 37-49) was a blessing wherever he went and favor followed him. Success is a natural outcome of being a blessing. Those who want to be a blessing don't fall into the fear of failure. The reason why some people are afraid to do the vision of making disciples is because they think they are going to fail. But make up your mind to be a blessing, if you don't, you will not free yourself from the pressure of failure. Stop trying to be successful and start trying being a blessing. The day you stop being a blessing, you start being a burden. But the day you start being a blessing, you stop being a burden.

What makes someone want to be blessing and what keeps a man from just wanting to be successful? It requires a *pure heart*. Only those with a pure heart can be a true blessing. Those without a pure heart will always have ulterior motives. Those who don't have a pure heart will end up with a divided heart. The proof of a pure heart is service. In fact, the fruit of a pure heart is service. Listen to what King Solomon said to the Lord in I Kings 3:8 "Your servant is in the midst of your great people..." He loved to serve and served to love. Remember, when reaching out to the lost, you can demonstrate your love for God by serving others.

At New Life, we have found many practical ways to be a blessing to our community and this has served as our most effective method of reaching souls. At least once a week, a cell group will go out together and set up a table. They will often serve free coffee or hot chocolate next to a bus stop or train station. It is amazing how receptive people become when you become a blessing to them. After they bless them, they collect contact information, such as names, phone numbers, emails, etc. Often they come back with 20 contacts within the first hour. You can win people's trust when you bless them and they see your loving heart at work. There are many ways you can be a blessing. You can ask God to give you creative ways to be a blessing in the target neighborhood you are trying to reach.

You Need a Net (Luke 5:4-7)

During the time of Jesus, fisherman would often use a net to catch many fish in one large catch. A large catch required the work of many people and good teamwork. To reach people for the Lord, team evangelism is critical. Team evangelism is accomplished through the strategy of *networks*. A network is a homogenous gathering of cell groups that work together to reach many for the

Lord at a given moment. The four basic Networks that we follow are the Men, Woman, Youth and Children Networks.

Network Meetings are conducted periodically to reach a large group of people for the Lord. Preparation is very important. It is essential that you start inviting people to the Network Meeting as soon as you hear that one has been scheduled. Don't wait until the last minute to invite someone or to motivate your cell group to invite people to the event. Also, keep in mind that you and your people will be inviting men, woman, or youths who come with a lot of baggage and issues. Many are blinded by sin, hurt, and in pain. As a disciple maker, you are to demonstrate excellence in whatever you present. Most people who come and visit a church come expecting a mediocre or substandard presentation. Excellence attracts and more importantly retains people who value it. Whenever you are asked to assist in any part of the Network Meeting, do it with a spirit of excellence. God's church should do everything with a five-star mentality. God deserves the best and it should reflect in everything we do in reaching souls.

Men of Power and Women of Substance

At New Life, the *Men of Power Network* meets periodically. We ask each of the men active in the cell groups, as well as church members, to bring at least one guest to the network meeting. This is *not* your typical men's fellowship meeting. It is an outreach event, designed to focus on reaching other men for God. In the Men of Power Network meetings, we have had a live worship band, an award winning Christian poet, the powerful testimony of a man reunited with his wife after seven years of separation, Christian rap, and messages from the Word which focuses on the contemporary needs of men. We spend time praying and laying hands on men who are in desperate need of Christ. By the end of the Network meeting, you will see the men you invited saved and reconcile to the Lord. While we see that the average church is lacking men, we have experienced occasional Sunday morning services where there have been more men than woman in attendance! The Men's Network has served to communicate to other men that serving God is a "man thing." If you are in the

Men's Network, this is a great way to start mobilizing your cell group into action. Set a goal in your heart as to how many men you will bring to the next Men's Network. The point of the network is to have a miracle catch. Bathe it with prayer and fasting. Let the Lord lead your conduct of each meeting. During the Men's Network, men maximize their manhood. It is not a time to beat them with shame and guilt. It is a time to deal with issues that today's man is confronting with the ultimate goal of winning them to the Lord.

Our Woman of Substance Network also meets on a periodic basis. The goal and the mission of the Woman's Network are similar to those of the Men's Network. Keep in mind that there is power in numbers. Crowds bring crowds. It is part of our culture. My wife and her G12 team conduct the meetings. Different leaders preach at each of the meetings. These meetings may involve a Fashion or Cosmetic Show, dealing with self-esteem or marriage/single life issues. The idea is to address areas of a women's lives, with the ultimate intent of touching their hearts with the power of the gospel.

The youth and children have their own network meeting that meet on a weekly basis. We hold the children's network during Sunday mornings and the youth on Friday evenings. The children's cell groups meet in what used to be Sunday School. The parents and church members conduct the lessons. The Youth Network Meeting is run entirely by the youth leaders and youth. The worship style music, message, drama and even announcements are tailor-made for today's youth.

You may ask, "Why divide them?" Networks *and* cell groups are organized homogenously to be better reach and heal each member of the family. If discipleship is done through role modeling, doesn't it make more sense that a woman could model and explain what a true woman of God is all about better than a man? How could a man better model a woman's character or what it means to live for Christ as a female? The opposite is also true. You can develop better husbands, wives, youth and children when you address like-minded issues and needs in a homogenous setting. This is not about splitting the family, it is about reaching the family one member at a time. The homogenous approach enables the church to focus the gospel message and outreach strategically to each member of the family. You are able to address certain needs in one network that may not be relevant to another network. People are able and tend to respond more openly in homogenous networks then they do in heterogeneous groups. Notice how Jesus himself, though He ministered to multitudes of women, selected only men for his group of twelve. It was a strategic approach.

When I meet with the men only groups, I can speak more openly about male-centered issues than when woman or children are present. The men don't have to put their "macho" guard up in the absence of the opposite sex and it allows for us to minister to the needs of the network without distractions and disruptions from other family members. We have seen families become stronger and healthier as a direct result of members attending the network meetings. As an example of this homogenous approach, the Bible tells us that "The older woman…admonish the young women to love their husbands, to love their children, to be discreet, chaste, homemakers, good, obedient to their husbands, that the word of God may not be blasphemed" (Titus 2:3-4).

City Wide Outreaches

We also use citywide outreaches as part of our "win souls" initiative. If evangelists Billy Graham, Victor Torres, Cesar Castellanos, or any other reputable evangelist comes to town, we have our cell group members invite their unbelieving friends and family members to these evangelistic events. When they give their lives to Jesus through these events, you as the group leader automatically consolidate those you took to the evangelistic outreach event within that week. These mass crusades can be an evangelistic catalyst to help you reach souls and see growth in your cell group.

Know What Type of Fish You are Going After

Jesus knew who He was after. He said, "I was sent only to the lost sheep of Israel" (Matt. 15:24). Paul in the other hand, focused on the Gentiles. It was not an issue of discrimination, but of strategy (see Matt. 10:5-6). Do you know the values, interests, fears and religious backgrounds of the people you are trying to reach? Sometimes the people you are trying to reach may not respond to your outreach because you may not be appealing to who they are and what they are looking for. Cell group leaders need to know whom exactly they are trying to reach. Also, keep in mind that most people go fishing for the type of fish they enjoy eating. In the same token, cell leaders usually reach out to those they can relate the best. We tend to attract what we are, not what we wish we were.

Use Various Tools of the Trade

Just like in sowing, you want to keep on learning new ways to improve your catching capability. Stay sharp on how to reach people through the combination of cell groups and celebration services. If you find some creative outreach strategy, continue doing what has worked for you before. If offering free coffee or chocolate by a train or bus station works for you, continue doing it. If going to the streets and inviting people works great for you, continue doing it. If witnessing in the train works for you, then continue doing it. If knocking at people's homes and inviting them to church works for you, continue doing it. If setting a prayer booth in front of a store works for you, continue doing it. Also, let me encourage you to learn from what other successful cell leaders are doing. With minor adjustments, they may work for your cell group. Some cell leaders have also put a lot of their energies around the big events days we have in our church such as Easter, Christmas, Father's Day, and Mother's Day. These events are designed to help you to present the gospel to your friends and family. Regardless of the strategy, find an approach that will connect you with the people you are trying to reach.

Learn to think like a fish thinks

The Bible says, "Jesus knew what they were thinking" (Matt. 9:4, 12:25). The problem with many Christians today is that the longer they live as a Christian, the more they forget what an unbeliever thinks like. Cell groups are not places for Christians to isolate themselves from unbelievers, but for unbelievers to get know and experience first hand what we have in Jesus. Get to know the interests of the person you are trying to reach. For example, if they are interested in improving their marriage, you will want to invite them to a Marriage Encounter.

Keep on fishing

It is always too soon to quit. Peter waited all night, but it was at the very last try and bidding of Jesus that he saw his miracle catch. True fishermen must be patient. In Elmer Towns' "Law of the Seven Touches", we learn that the average person will usually make a decision to follow Christ after the church has contacted the person seven times. If they don't respond the first time, continue reaching out. You may be just one invitation away from winning that person to the Lord. It is the "seed – water – growth" principle that we find in I Corinthians 3:6, where Paul says, "I planted, Apollos watered, but God was causing the growth." Many times, winning a person to the Lord is a process rather than a one-time event. So don't be discouraged if they don't respond in a positive manner the first time you invite a person to come to church or you share the gospel with them. Keep on watering the Word you planted in them. In due season, you will reap what you have sown. Many times I have witnessed how a family member was initially unsuccessful at the beginning in reaching their family, but after staying the course and not giving up, his or her family members eventually came to Jesus.

Keep your focus on the goal

The Great Commission, detailed in Matthew 28:18-19, tells us that winning souls is necessary because God desires it and man needs it. The Great Commission is the obligation of the church; it is not an option. Disciple makers understand that they will never be "unemployed" in the kingdom of God as long there is a soul that needs conversion and salvation. When you understand that winning souls is your purpose, a fire for souls will come upon your heart and soul. This is the same fire Jesus experienced. The Great Commission is not a calling upon a select few, but a personal call upon every one who considers themselves a disciple of Jesus.

Cell leaders use a variety of methods to win souls

Be a Blessing: Find a way to be a blessing to the community. This is the best way to gain instant credibility with the community members and neighborhood. Find something you want to bless the community with (example: coffee, cake, cold water in the summer heat, etc.). You begin to be a blessing sharing in a busy area of your community with those who pass by.

Flyers: The most effective flyer distribution is the one that is accompanied by a personal invitation. The great thing about flyers and invitation cards is that they are a lasting reminder to the person you are inviting to an event. A radio or television commercial lasts for only 30 seconds to a minute. Invitation cards, in the other hand, have a lasting impact. I have seen people come to church only after forgetting about the initial invitation, but remembering about a special evangelistic event when looking at the invitation card, which was given to the person. Or they received a flyer at one time and then visited the church when they were faced a difficult time in their lives.

The Prayer of Three: We are told in John 4:37 that "One sows and another reaps." In other words, evangelism requires teamwork. One of the most effective tools in winning souls and making disciples is the prayer of three. What is the prayer of three? The prayer of three is when your core group of three people gets together to pray *daily,* for a period of a month, to pray for nine people. Each of the three group members presents three names, for a total of nine people who need the Lord. They pray for receptivity. They pray for a month that the Holy Spirit create a spiritual hunger and thirst in these nine who need the Lord (I Timothy 2:1). At the end of the month, those who prayed the prayer of three go to the three people they presented with an invitation to attend their cell group or Sunday celebration service. The goal is for all nine to receive the Lord and become active group members. Someone once asked me, "Do you think that the prayer of three works?" I responded, "Well, let me ask you a question, 'Do you think that someone will be more receptive after three people have prayed for that person daily for a whole month, or if the person was approached 'cold turkey' without intercession being made for that person?" The answer was obvious.

The following is a suggested pattern for implementing the prayer of three:

Week #1: Find two people in your cell group who will interchange 3 names of people who need the Lord. Commit yourselves to pray for these nine people for a period of four weeks. Ask God that He will grant mercy. Pray for them as if you were asking God for mercy for yourself (Daniel 9:5). Ask the Lord to convict them of their sins (John 16:8) and that God will destroy the work of Satan in their lives.

Week #2: Establish communication and contact with the three you pray for. Continue in daily prayer for them.

Week #3: Show interest in their needs and dreams and continue in your prayer regimen.

Week #4: After four weeks of prayer and contact efforts, invite them to your cell group or celebration service.

Prayer is no substitute for evangelism. Don't just pray the prayer of three and then neglect to evangelize. It is much easier to talk to God about men than to talk to men about God.

Go in the power of the Holy Spirit, now having prayed, and win you friends and family to the Lord.

Inviting someone to the Encounter

The Encounter is a great place for a person to meet Christ as a Savior and Deliverer. I have had many unbelievers accept my invitation to an Encounter Weekend. Most of the people that do come do so primarily to deal with an inner hurt or pain. Just make sure that they have gone through the Pre-Encounter, which will be discussed later in the book. During the Encounter they are given an opportunity to receive Jesus as their Lord and Savior.

Empty Chair

Every week in your group, leave an empty chair available. The empty chair raises the level of consciousness needed to reach the lost on a weekly basis. The basic question you will be asking your cell group members is: "Who are you going to invite next week?" Teach your group members not to rely on only one or two verbal commitments by friends and family, but increase their possibilities by asking at least five to ten people to attend the group.

Lifestyle Evangelism

Listen with compassion to the person you are trying to reach. Build rapport and establish a relationship with the person you are trying to reach. Share spiritual answers to the issues, problems and needs in his or her life. Then, pray for those issues that the person is facing. Once God answers your prayers, invite them to receive Jesus as Lord and Savior. Invite the new convert to your cell group.

Friendship Evangelism

In this type of outreach, you reach out to friends through fellowship and a "friendship" event. You may choose to invite them to a "Bring a Friend Luncheon," Jesus Video, or picnic. The idea is for your friends to invite them to a seeker-friendly event to build trust and assimilate them into your group by connecting through other group members.

Chapter Three: Consolidate through Reaching

We not only called to reach out, but to keep the souls God has entrusted to us. In order to keep someone who has come to Christ, we must consolidate them. The word consolidate speaks of a soldier who takes over a hill during battle and sets up a perimeter in order to prevent the enemy from repossessing what he has lost. The goal of consolidation is to keep those disciples you have already won for the Lord. Consolidation is an effective and efficient process for making disciples and "solidifying" those you have already won to the Lord. Consolidation is the attention and shepherding we should give a new born-again believer in order to reproduce the character of Christ in him. Consolidation is used to close the back door of the church. We accomplish consolidation through mentorship.

Mentors Needed!

Every disciple maker is a mentor. A disciple maker must develop a heart of mentor. It is an inner attitude that says, "No matter what it takes, I am going to reach out to this new believer and disciple him with all my heart." A true mentor understands that consolidation is the thread to the net in retaining new believers. I once heard a disciple maker say to me, "I prayed for forgiveness for each person I did not consolidate." A mentor burns with a passion for those who may be lost due to the negligence of the lack of follow up. *A true mentor and consolidator will never give up on reaching a guest or new believer that has been assigned to him or her.* Good intentions without paying the price of consolidation are dangerous. A consolidator is not satisfied with merely wishing a new believer well, but in doing every thing possible to strengthen and present the new believer blameless before the Lord.

Every mentor must believe that the moment they enter the home of a new believer or guest, they bring transformation with them. A mentor enters the house of a new believer with the belief that he is a difference maker. Consolidators prepare themselves through prayer before attending a home. They ask God for wisdom and a "rhema" and timely word for the person they are visiting. They understand that there will be no real change unless they have spent time in prayer. They come with no hidden agenda. They radiate an ambiance of authenticity and realness. Consolidators focus on one thing: NEEDS. They are not afraid to deal with personal issues and needs.

A true consolidator is concerned about the disciple's character formation. He is conscious that the new disciple will learn, hear and see what Christ is like through his demeanor and actions (Philippians 4:9). Character is the wellspring of discipleship. Without character formation, there will be no true compassion. Without compassion, you can't have effective consolidation.

What does the heart of consolidator look like?

The heart of a consolidator is the heart of a father or mother (Galatians 4:19). In the heart of every parent there is an innate vigilance for his or her children to always make it home safely. What would you say of a father who leaves home to the mall with five children and comes home with four? Imagine this father saying, "I only lost one, I still have four." It would be a crime for a father to think in these terms. A true father would spend all of attention, time, and effort to find that child which is missing. The same is true with spiritual children. A true spiritual father or mother is as intense to consolidate as he was to win.

Take a look how in Galatians 4:19 Paul says, "My little children, of whom I travail in birth again until Christ be formed in you..." Notice the words "...I am again..." He was intense in the painful *process* of winning, and now he is intense in the painful *process* of consolidating. Consolidation is like giving birth. Without pain there will be no consolidation. It is the pain of a mother who wants the best for her child. It is the pain of a mother who wants the child to make it and grow to be healthy. Without experiencing the labor birth of consolidation, there will be no character formation. In Isaiah 23:4, God says, "Be ashamed, O Sidon, for the sea has spoken, the strength of the sea, saying, '*I do not labor, nor bring forth children*; neither do I rear young men, nor bring up virgins." If there is no labor, there will be no children. A consolidator is like a true father, who sees the full potential in the child. They are able to say to the child, "I see you in your full potential." A consolidator loves their disciples as their own sons. Fathers beget sons. Keep this in mind: if you don't consolidate your sons and daughters in the Lord, your sons will not consolidate. Never accept that you will lose the fruit of sons and daughters the Lord has for you.

Just like a mother who is pregnant who travails, so a consolidator will travail in seeing Christ formed in the heart of a new disciple. There is no birth without travail (Genesis 3:16). The prophet Isaiah said it like this: "As soon as Zion travailed, she brought forth children" (Isaiah 66:8). A consolidator will at times agonize in his or her spirit regarding the new believer. Nehemiah groaned for the condition he found the people of God in (Nehemiah 1:1-9). A consolidator carries the souls of the disciples entrusted upon him in his heart. I like the way John Wesley says it, "The love of Christ doth me constrain to seek the wandering souls of men; with cries, entreaties, tears, to save, to snatch them from the fiery wave." His heart was bursting with a desire for souls to make it.

Travail entails work. Apostle Paul put it this way, "For ye remember, brethren, our labor and travail: for laboring night and day, because we would not be chargeable unto any of you, we preached unto you the gospel of God" (I Thessalonians 2:9). If there is no labor, there is no lasting fruit. God does not commit his newborn children to people who do not care to see conversions and care for the growth of people who are in need of Christ. Who is so fit to encourage a newborn believer as the man who first anguished before the Lord for his conversion? Charles Spurgeon, the great British pastor of the 19th century, best describe the type of heart

God is looking for in the consolidator when he said, "The work would go on without the mass of you, Christians; many of you only hinder the march of the army; but give us a dozen lion-like, lamb-like men, burning with intense love to Christ and souls, and nothing will be impossible to their faith."

We have a fatherless society. Often, people experience a father vacuum. It is a wound of absence or neglect. Disciples need this type of spiritual experience in their lives (I Corinthians 4:14). Great men and women of God were afforded this type of opportunity. Elisha, before the Lord took up Elijah, his leader and mentor, said, "My father, father, the chariots of Israel and its horsemen." Remember, it was Elisha who received a double portion of what Elijah had. He performed twice as many miracles that his mentor Elijah did. This is how disciples grow; that is, through fatherhood. The anointing of God increases in the lives of disciples through spiritual fathering.

There are five pillars of fathering and mothering. The first is *protection*. Every believer has a blind spot. We all have areas of our lives that where we are unaware, which is hurting our walk with God. Spiritual fathers and mothers are there to help new disciples from hurting themselves spiritually and emotionally. As trust is established, a new disciple begins to grant access to their issues and personal struggles. New believers are like children; they will go where they are not supposed to go. And just like biological children, spiritual children will feel insecure if no one is watching over them. It should be clarified that protection does not mean control. Protection also does not mean enabling. Never do for a disciple what they can do for themselves.

Fathering also involves *correction*. When there is no correction, the child is not validated. Just like biological children, children feel like they belong and are connected when they are held accountable. Once, in a place in the jungles of Africa, many rhinoceroses were dying. They got a specialist and found out that the young elephants were going after the rhinos and attacking them. The specialist also found that there were no adult elephants

44

present among these young elephants. They brought three adult elephants to mingle with these young elephants. The next time the young elephants charged a young rhinoceros, the big and grown elephant corrected the young elephant by charging against him. Never again did the young elephants charge against the rhinoceros. They learned respect through the mature and grown elephants. In the church, new converts have the potential of bullying each other. Spiritual parents are there to correct actions when necessary. They ask the question, *"What are you doing?"* In the bible, we find that David was a great king, but a lousy father. His son Absalom had violated his half sister. But as a father, he never confronted nor corrected his son about it. He never asked his son Absalom, "What are you doing?" Who has the right to ask you, "What are you doing?" A spiritual father or mother has the right and obligation to ask you this question. As a spiritual parent to the new convert, you have the God given responsibility to ask your son and daughter in the Lord, "What are you doing?" And, you know you have become a spiritual parent when are granted permission to ask this very question. In Hebrews 12:5, we are told that God disciplines. It goes on to explain that true fathers discipline because they love their children.

The third pillar is *direction*. Fathering involves giving input into the life of a son or daughter. In I Corinthians 4:14, we are told that a disciple may have many "instructors." The Greek word for "instructors" is the word for babysitters. The church in America today has the same problem. It has assumed a baby-sitting role. Churches have often become spiritual baby-sitting centers. They provide spiritual information, but no spiritual formation. We were called to develop as fully devoted disciple. We can settle with just having church attendees, but experience no transformation. We can provide a tremendous amount of guidance through modeling. Modeling is a form of direction. Fathering and mothering it is not just what I tell you to do, but also what you watch me to do. Your example as a disciple maker is important.

The fourth pillar is *affirmation*. New disciples need a tremendous amount of validation. Even God the Father validated His son Jesus when He said to Him at His baptism, "This is my beloved Son." Jesus had not done a miracle yet. And yet, God the Father affirmed him. Affirmation occurs through relationships. Until you as a spiritual father or mother affirm your disciple, he or she will spend their entire walk with God seeking approval. Keep in mind that you don't dig up jewels off the ground. You have to dig deep and take off all the debris and junk off of it to get to the jewel. Fathering and mothering in the Lord is looking at a disciple as a jewel. In Malachi 3:17, the Lord gave us an example of affirmation when He said, "'They will be Mine,' says the Lord of Hosts, 'on the day that I prepare My own possession, and I will spare them as a man spares his own son who serves him.'"

The fifth pillar is *modeling*. Just like earthly parents do, spiritual parents show us how to live. Disciples need strong leaders to show them how to handle the issues of life. Spiritual parents are the kind of people who make us want to be like them. Dr. John Maxwell, in speaking about mentors, says, "We teach what we know, but reproduce what we are." Mentors win the hearts of their disciples through their example. Rusty Caldwell said it best when it comes to modeling:

"I do; you watch
I do; you help
You do; I help
You do: I watch
You know
We do it together as a team!"

The heart of a consolidator is the heart of a faithful shepherd (John 17:12 "I guarded them"). This is the attitude of a true shepherd: "I will not lose one." A true consolidator loves the sheep. It is not just a matter of getting them to the Encounter and Post-Encounter, but mentoring, shepherding, and loving them through it. It is not just the mechanics of discipleship, but having a heartbeat for those you are ministering to. Please don't lose this point, because otherwise discipleship will become a duty and not a delight. Consolidation is about establishing a mentoring relationship. I remember once that a youth consolidator in Mission Charismatic International in Bogotá, related to me that he had a dream that the Lord was rescuing people from the mud and would pass it on to the army (leaders and disciple makers), but the disciple makers would not take care of them and would lose them. If someone has to go constantly motivate you to go consolidate the "sheep", it tells me that you are not going after the sheep. In Acts 14:21 we are told that "after they had preached the gospel to that city and had made many disciples, they *returned* to Lystra and to Iconium and to Antioch, *strengthening* the souls of the disciples, *encouraging* them to continue in the faith..." Do you see the heart of the consolidator in them, returning time after time to strengthen them and encourage them in the Lord? Keep in mind, they did not have cars, the Internet, telephones and other means of connecting conveniently with the disciples. But they did have something we often lack in churches – the heart of the consolidator.

The heart of the consolidator is the heart of a fighter. You have to fight for what God has given you. You have to fight for your sons and daughters in the Lord like a lion fights for his cubs. You must learn to do spiritual warfare for your men or women. A consolidator is not passive. He is constantly active to make sure that their disciples are making it. In II Corinthians 10:1-4, we are told that consolidators break the partitions. The word used in most Bibles, appearing in verse two, is "stronghold." The word "stronghold' means "to harden, or to make hard." It describes an entrenchment or fortress. Thus, in the spiritual life, Paul is speaking of a hard place. He is speaking of an unbending place. He is speaking of an area contended for such as an entrenchment behind the lines. It is anything that poses a threat to your disciple's spiritual progress. It is any person, place, predicament, or problem that hinders, harbors, or holds your disciples in their spiritual and emotional clutches and impedes them from their full potential in Christ. A.W. Tozer once said that a vast majority of Christians believe that the world is a playground instead of a battleground. What makes up this fortress? What impedes most of your disciples from fully growing and serving Christ is was Paul calls an "argument". An argument is a thought or "voice" in our mind that comes against what Christ wants us to do or believe. It may be the voice of fear, rejection, insecurity, shame, or sin. It seeks to dethrone the supremacy of Christ and to make him less important than he is. There is an argument for every lifestyle that is contrary to the holiness of God. There is an argument for every sin that is controlling a new believer's life. These arguments fire back at those who are being bulldozed with the truth in love. We find an example of an argument holding someone back in Acts 8:18-24. We are told that bitterness was blinding Simon. He was being motivated by a thought (he had a stronghold). He had accepted that particular thought as his own and acted on it. It was just *one* thought. We have been called as consolidators and disciple makers to dethrone every thought that is not of Christ in our disciples. If you don't fight for your people and have them move through discipleship, sooner or later you will loose them. Strongholds are broken in the Pre-Encounter, Encounter, Post-Encounter and School of Disciple Makers. But they are also broken through your mentorship and by getting your disciples involved within the life of the church. This is why it is also so important to have your people get into the Word and not just your Bible studies. It is the Word that will set them free.

The heart of the consolidators is the heart of a watchman. In Jeremiah 31:6 God put it this way, "For there will be a day when watchmen on the hills of Ephraim call out, 'Arise, and let us go to Zion, To the Lord our God.'" As a disciple maker, you have been called to watch over the souls of the disciples entrusted to you by the Lord. Paul guarded his disciples as a father who watches protectively over his daughter before she is given in marriage to her future husband. Paul wants the church, engage to Christ, to remain faithful to her future husband (Eph. 5:27 "without wrinkle or blemish in holiness and purity").

Reproduce who you are

(I Cor. 4:16 "be imitators of me") As a disciple maker, God has done incredible things in your life. He is changing you and transforming you. Now it is time to pass it on to others. Did you know that the development and mentoring of half of the head coaches in the NFL in 1998 could be traced to two outstanding former pro football leaders – Bill Walsh and Tom Landry? It takes a leader to raise a leader. It takes a disciple maker to raise a disciple maker. So, the day you start seeing yourself as a disciple maker is the day that you will start reproducing the disciple maker in you. Yes, it is the disciple maker God has developed in your through the ministry of the leader God has placed in your life. This is why as a disciple maker you need to make it a point to grow. If you grow, others will want what you have. People naturally follow leaders stronger than themselves. You cannot give to others what you do not possess yourself. You may say, "I don't have much." But, you do have something and what you have, many others do not have. And the more you are quick to give it away, the more God will give you. Remember, people buy into the leader more then the vision. People will not buy into the vision until you, as the leader, do the vision. If you consolidate them properly, your disciples will take notice of it and connect with you. No one doubts that David, the man who killed Goliath, was a great leader. What few people know is that no fewer than five of the leaders he developed were giant killers. *The heart of the consolidator is the heart of a mentor.*

What is mentorship?

Mentorship is the most intimate and practical means to impart the vision and character of Jesus upon someone else. It involves building a legacy that never ends. You will only be remembered by what you impart in others. Your impact to reach this world will only last to the degree you impart unto others. As a disciple maker, keep in mind that mentorship is a *priority*. It is not one of the many things we do in church; it is the main thing we do in church. Mentorship is not about a program, but about investing in people. It is a mindset and lifestyle where you pass on what God has passed on to you. Mentorship is not about control or manipulation. It is about establishing a godly relationship in developing a disciple into a disciple maker.

Mentoring is helping people go to where they need to be in the Lord from where they are now. Mentors teach what is effective and efficiency in reaching this world for God. A mentor will work through with what they got in their disciple to develop a disciple maker. Mentors recognize that just because a disciple has been called of God to make disciples does not guarantee they will automatically become a disciple maker. Mentors help the protégée stay focused so that they may stay on the path of become a disciple maker. Mentors are not into accommodating the past, but preparing for the future of their protégée. Mentors help their disciple finish what they have started.

THE BENEFITS OF MENTORSHIP

You get to reap a harvest from the seed you plan in your protégée.

Your protégée is an extension of you. He is able to reach places and people that you were not able to reach. You, as a mentor, serve to help your trainee reach his destiny in multiplication. Your goal is to impart the knowledge and experience to help your protégée avoid the pitfalls of ministry. Your mission is to help your protégée avoid the wrong "harbors" and turns in the midst of their storm and trials.

THE PURPOSE OF MENTORSHIP

God will place people in your cell group to be developed as disciple makers. God will connect you to the right people at the right time for the right purpose. God placed Timothy into Paul's path for the purpose of developing him into a leader who would reach multitudes. Sometimes people miss the purpose of God in their lives because they do not get connected with the mentor God has placed in their path. God is in the business of connecting people who make themselves available to be mentored. At times it may seem that the process of making disciples is slow, but often it means that God is getting you connected with the people who will follow the vision of making disciples. God knows how to pair you off with the right person. He knows how to match others with you who are in need of mentorship.

God uses mentorship to birth a future for your protégée that will bring many to the Lord.

As a cell leader, God will connect you with people to help them fulfill their destiny as a child of God. He uses relationships to connect people to become what God has purposed in their lives. The devil will at times attempt to disconnect you from those whom you are discipling. He knows that if he can disconnect you from those in your cell group, mentorship will not take place. Where there is no mentorship, there will be no disciples. Where there are no disciples, there will be no one to reap the harvest of souls. Notice how Hamon attempted to sabotage the mentorship relationship Modercai had with Esther (Esther 3). But we find God protecting the mentor and keeping the mentorship relationship alive. The devil knows that if Esther had disconnected from her mentor Mordacai, she would have not fulfilled her God-given destiny, which literally saved and touched thousands of her people. The devil fears mentorship. Mentorship creates a connection that will impart godly wisdom. The kingdom of God grows rapidly and effectively when you are imparting the wisdom He has imparted unto you. The devil does not want you to impart wisdom and that is why he will attempt to disrupt and disconnect your mentorship relationships with those who will be or are in your cell group.

Second, God uses mentorship to increase the level of excellence that will result in multiplication.

Your job as a mentor is to uproot mediocrity in those under your mentorship. When people come to the Lord, they often come with bad habits that result in little fruit in their lives. As a mentor, you have the privilege to train your people to do the work of God in a spirit of excellence. What we do, we do for the Lord. He deserves the best. Your job is to train the people how to give their best for God. If you love those whom God has given you to mentor, you will want to influence them to change and not stay the same. Effective mentors push their people lovingly to excellence.

Third, mentorship is the most effective way of helping someone launch his or her assignment from God.

Every believer has been called to make disciples, but not every believer does it well or at all. Mentors motivate their protégée to fulfill the Great Commission and Great Commandment. Mentorship speeds up the process of people fulfilling their God-given assignment. Mentorship is about impartation and investing into someone's life. Mentorship imparts the ability someone needs to fulfill his or her destiny. When you spend time imparting your knowledge and experience, it helps to accelerate the discipleship process to launch someone to go and make disciples. There are people who go through life unable to fulfill the Great Commission effectively, because they lack mentorship in their lives. Mentorship helps your cell group members to go about making disciples efficiently and effectively. The more you connect with your group members, the more momentum you will see in the direction of fulfilling the Great Commission.

Fourth, mentorship helps your group members increase their credibility.

People in the world tend to judge others by whom they associate with. Others will open doors to your protégée because of your credibility and integrity. Many times, doors will only open for your protégée based on your word of integrity. Even more important, their credibility is increased when their integrity is developed through mentorship. People connect with those who demonstrate the type of character that can be trusted.

Fifth, mentors help group members reach their goals.

They help their people decipher goals that are believable and achievable. True mentors assist their protégée in seeing what is achievable today and attainable next year. As a mentor, you will be helping group members sort out the right timing. This may include deciding when to open your protégée's cell group or when to embark in an outreach event to help the group grow. At times you may find your protégée struggling with impulsivity, so help them to respect God's tempo in their lives. Your job is to help your protégée decide what is necessary for now and possible for later. There will be other cell group members that may lag behind in reaching their goal and need a gentle infusion of enthusiasm from you.

Sixth, mentors focus in developing growth and maturity.

Cell group member who don't grow in maturity are a liability and dangerous in ministry. Character is essential in avoiding the pitfalls of ministry. Character is essential in reaching multitudes of souls. Character is essential in becoming a leader of leaders. As a mentor, focus on shaping maturity among your group members. The faster they mature, the quicker they will develop into your group of 12 disciple makers. If you bypass this purpose of mentorship, you will find yourself dealing with a lot pain and suffering from a leader who is out of control later on. An immature leader can be potentially dangerous to people who may attending his/her cell group.

Seven, mentorship produces successors who will carry on the work of God.

The message and teachings of the gospel will continue to reach multitudes when we develop disciples. In II Timothy 2:2, you are instructed to entrust what has been imparted upon you to faithful men and woman. God will not just judge you based on what you did in the present, but what you left for the future. The beauty of the vision of the groups of 12 is that your work will outlive you. From generation to generation, what you did for the Lord will continue years after you have gone to be with the Lord. Men like John Wesley, having established over 10,000 cell groups, gave birth to the Methodist denomination. And his legacy has continued long after his death. When you invest in others it will outlast you.

Every leader you will develop in your group of 12 disciple makers will in turn pass on what you have invested in them and so on. What a marvelous opportunity you have to touch countless of people, even after you have gone to be with the Lord!

It is a privilege and duty to mentor someone, but you need a mentor too.

How to get the most out of your mentor

You need a mentor who knows your name. Jesus said in John 10:3 that "he calls his own sheep by name". It is easy to come to church and feel lost. One of our church members said that he came to our church and liked it. But what impressed him the most was the following week someone called him by his name. From that day forward he decided to stay. You need someone who knows your voice. Did you know that you voice is as distinct to you as a fingerprint? It is one of a kind. No one ever in the history of mankind ever spoke with the exact same voice as you. Here are the questions you need to ask: "are you known?" and "are you letting people know you?"

You need a mentor who watches out for wolves. In John 10:10, Jesus warns us "the thief comes to steal, kill and destroy". There are two kinds of wolves. The first are the thieves. They come to steal sheep. False religions and cults are more aggressive than ever in recruiting new converts into their flocks. You need someone who will teach you and protect you from those who will seek to pull you out of the flock of God. Then we have the "hirelings". The hirelings are those who have a hidden agenda of why they are helping you. These are the ones who consider themselves "private prophets" and who are not under authority. There is nothing wrong with someone wanting to go to another church, but there is something wrong when someone goes into another church to actively recruit members from it.

You need mentor who look out for you. In John 10:11, we are told, "the good shepherd lays down his life for the sheep". You need someone who is looking out for your best interest.
The "hired hand" is not "concerned" (v.13). In Ezekiel 34, we are told that shepherds seek and search for lost sheep.

You need a mentor so he/she can feed you. In Ezekiel 34:2, we are asked "…should not be shepherds feed the flock?" (Ez. 34:2). By the way, shepherds should feed you what you need, not what you may want. You need someone to speak into your life. You need someone when you are broken and sick (Ez. 34:16). There will be times when the wild beasts will slash you and bruise you. In this age, more than ever, you need someone to care for your needs.

Your mentor see what you see, but from a different viewpoint. The reason why your mentor can see from a different point of view is because your mentor has been where you are already. Please understand that your mentor's goal is not to kill your joy, but to help you fulfill the plan of God in your life. Ruth met Boaz, but it took Naomi, her mentor, to prepare her to see the purpose of God fulfilled. Many people mess things up because they choose not to listen to the mentors God has placed in their lives. God works through mentors to help you see situations, problems and opportunities in your cell group from a different angle. When you have a mentor, it will profit everyone in your group and lead you into multiplication. It takes a mentor who has been where you are going to help you get there. The mentor God has placed in your life knows what it is to start a cell group from scratch and see it grow. Your mentor has already experience the fears and frustrations that you may be experiencing right now as a new cell group leader.

Be faithful and loyal. The proof that you have submitted to mentorship is longevity. Faithfulness and loyalty is a sign that you have understood the value of mentorship from your mentor.

You need to realize that you need your mentor.   In the day you feel that you don't need your mentor, you are walking on dangerous ground. The disciples had Jesus as a mentor. Elisha had an Elijah as a mentor. Timothy had a Paul for a mentor. Ruth had a Naomi for a mentor. Esther had a Mordecai for a mentor. Great woman and men of God have mentors.

You need to connect with your mentor. You need to "pursuit" your cell group leader for wisdom, knowledge, strategies, and friendship. How much you pursuit your mentor will determine how connected you will be. Your mentor is looking to see how hungry you are to learn and to grow as a disciple of Jesus. There are no short cuts. Spend time with your mentor. Call your mentor. Attend the activities and meetings your mentor sets up.

Be teachable, bendable and sendable. Your mentor has much to teach you. Your mentor has already gone through the struggles and joys of starting a new group. Your mentor has learned what not do to.   Learn to be flexible and open to suggestions. Remember, you mentor has the best in mind for you. Your mentor selected you because he or she saw you as teachable, bendable, and sendable.

Promotion is never achieved by doing the work alone. God blesses those who work together. The work of reaching multitudes for Christ is too big for one person to do alone. God expects us to operate under the basis of partnership. God has linked you to your mentor to see increase and promotion in your life.

Spend time with your mentor. If you spend quality time with your mentor, you will develop a quality ministry. There is no substitute to spending valuable time with your cell leader.

The Importance of a Home Visit
Effective mentors perform home visits. It is very important that if you are going to reach and keep disciples that you learn the importance and practical aspects of making a home visit. We find in I Thessalonians 2:1 that Paul visited people's homes in order to

make sure that the souls he won to the Lord remained within the body of Christ. Paul said, "Our coming to you was not in vain". There is something very powerful in doing a home visit. Even salesmen know the power of getting inside through the door of a house. Paul, in this passage, talked about returning to visit them. Often, we find Paul grieving when he could not visit his newly developed disciples. Some new disciple makers at times fail to initially see the value of doing a home visit. But we find that though Paul had a full-time job, he still visited people's homes. He knew that it was not wasted time. But how did he come to this conclusion? Paul felt the impact of a home visit when he first got saved. We find in Acts 9 that Ananias came and paid him a home visit soon after he came to a revelation of Jesus. Even though Ananias knew what kind of a man Paul was, he still did a home visit because he was a man of obedience. Think about it; he went on a home visit to someone who everyone knew to be a killer of Christians. He took a risk. Now, he did not go into the home visit saying, "I am here just because I need to obey," but he ministered to Paul out of love and concern. It was during this visit with Annaias that Paul received the baptism of the Holy Spirit. Imagine if Ananias had not been obedient and not done a home visit?

Home visits are the key to consolidation

Home visits bring about many benefits in developing a new believer into a disciple. First, when you make a home visit, they experience acceptance. Often, people feel unworthy to be visited by a leader or disciple maker. Do you remember the centurion when he told Jesus, "I am not worthy for you to come into my house"? A home visit causes a new born believer to say to himself, "I am important to this person."

When you do a home visit, you are bestowing honor to your cell member. When you do a home visit you are honoring the new born-again believer with your presence. Second, you have an opportunity to fortify relationships. The times my wife and I have made home visit have allowed us to bond with the new believer. It allows you to know them in more intimate way then you would otherwise have known them before or after a church service. Also, it allows them to know you and connect with you in a more meaningful way. I guarantee you that you will see them in a different light after you made that home visit. Third, it allows you to take Jesus into their homes. How else do we take Jesus their homes? People need a visitation of Jesus. You are a representative of Christ and an ambassador of Heaven. When you go to people's home, you take Jesus with you. When Jesus came into people homes, they experienced change. When you take Jesus to their homes, expect transformation to occur. Next, a home visit allows you to minister through miracles and the anointing. We often see Jesus and the disciples performing greater miracles in people's homes than in the temple. Did you know that we find only four recorded miracles taking place in the temple and the rest took place in people's home and in the street? When you do a home visit, you are taking the presence of the Holy Spirit into someone's home. The Bible tells us that when the Ark of the Covenant ended up at Obed's home that Obed and his household was blessed. The Ark of the Covenant is representative of us. We now carry the presence of God. And wherever you go, you bring in the power of the presence of God.

The attitude of the Mentor who visits

Be concerned as a father is for his son. A father and mother always have a healthy preoccupation with the condition of their children. In I Thessalonians 2:1, Paul was concerned that they would be discouraged. He was concerned that his disciples would be tempted and his winning work would be in vain. He put it this way in I Thessalonians 3:5: "For this reason, when I could endure it no longer, I also sent to find out about your faith, for fear that the tempter might have tempted you, and our labor would be in vain." Consolidation involves fathering and mothering your disciples (I Corinthians 4).

Be prepared for Satanic opposition to home visit. So important is the home visit that Satan comes against it. Satan understands the value of a home visit in solidifying a new believer's faith in the

58

Lord. He will tells you lies, such as, "They don't want you to come to their home", "It is so intrusive", "How about if they reject you?" or "You don't have time to do home visits." Paul did not allow Satanic opposition to deter him from making a home visit.

People want you to come. Notice what it says in I Thessalonians 3:6, "Longing to see us just as we also long to see you." They desired for Paul to come. Many times a new leader will reject himself from doing a home visit, while the new disciples is "longing" for their cell leader to come to their homes. People want you to come because you matter to them. They are also full of questions that need to be answered. Keep in mind that you are a representative of the church and this matters greatly to people today.

There is no substitute for your face to show up. We are told in I Thessalonians 3:10 that, "As we night and day keep praying most earnestly that we may see your face, and may complete what is lacking in your faith." Emails, letters, and phone calls are important steps in bonding with a new disciple. But there is no substitute for a face-to-face meeting. New disciples need to see your facial expression and countenance. Initially, your face communicates the love of God and acceptance like nothing else. Your face sends a message.

Invite yourself. Jesus did! He invited himself to Matthew's house right after he experienced conversion. Mathew even invited his sinner friends to be present. Jesus did the same thing with Zaccheus. Jesus told him, "Today..." He did not procrastinate or put off visiting this new disciple. In the midst of all the important things Jesus had to do, He made priority number one to visit his home that day.

If you love people you will love home visits. If you say you really love someone and yet do not visit him or her, your love lacks something. It is a special moment when I visit my daughter Lissette and her husband Carlos in their home. Why? It is because I love them dearly. The same is true with our spiritual children.

Practical aspects of a home visitation

People are most opened for a home visit in the midst of a crisis. People make themselves most vulnerable when confronting trials or facing transitions. Don't say, "They don't want to be bothered." What you need to realize is that you are not bothering anyone; rather, you are connecting with people in their time of need. That is exactly what Jesus did.

Show up with something in your hands. Remember the home visit by the three kings, who came with gifts for Jesus and his family. The three kings came to Joseph and Mary in a time of economic distress. At the very least you want to come with a Pre-Encounter book that the church makes available for you to give to the new convert.

Speak of what is good. When the angel showed up to Mary at her home, he said, "Greetings, favored one! The Lord is with you... Mary, for you have found favor with God" (v.28-30). During a home visit, it is not time to speak negativity or criticize. It is a time to speak words of edification (Ephesians 4:30). Ask yourself, "What can I speak unto this new convert's life that will strengthen his or her faith?" As a cell leader, you never want to complain in front of your disciples. Praises go down, complaints go up!

Move in the supernatural. In Acts 9:39, we are told that Peter raised the dead in the upper room of someone's home. In Acts 10:44, the Spirit of God was poured out while he was speaking at Cornelius' house. Do not be afraid to believe God for the supernatural. People today need miracles in their homes. Unto you as a disciple of Jesus has been given authority and power to do the works of God.

Sacrifice comfort. At times, it may be an inconvenience to visit someone's home. But keep in mind that Jesus left the comfort of his home to visit our home that we may have life (Phil. 2:5). If Jesus did it for us, and He gave up greater comfort, joy, and peace, how much more should we follow his example? When you visit someone at his or her home, you are imitating your Lord Jesus.

Why should a church member or visitor join a cell group?

Since many people who you will come in contact with have never been in a cell group, you will often find yourself asked this question: why they should join or even visit a cell group? People pursue what they value. So it makes sense to share with people the value of attending a cell group. Let us take some time at this moment to list the main reasons for attending a cell group.

The disciple will understand the Word of God better in a small group. Have you ever listened to a teacher or preacher and wanted to stop that person and say, "But what about...?" or "I don't understand!" It is in a small group setting that we learn the best. In a small group setting disciples are able to have two-way communication with their cell leader. In preaching and teaching, you will find often only one-way communication. The disciple only gets to listen while the speaker lectures. Preaching and teaching are excellent modes of communication for sharing knowledge but not as successful for personal application as small groups. In a cell group setting, a disciple can ask questions, participate in a discussion about a particular passage of Scripture, and learn from others in the group who have something beneficial to share. The Bible was meant to be a book of application, and this occurs best in a small group setting.

The disciple will experience bonding with the church. Christianity is about relationships. And close relationships best happen in a small group. It is easy to feel lost in a large congregational setting. But in a small group, the group members frequently telephone each other during the week to encourage one another. They soon discover that their needs, and trials are often experienced by everyone else. It is a good feeling to know that others have made it through the same problem by utilizing biblical principles. The New Testament uses the phrase "one another" over 50 times to describe our relationship to other believers. We are instructed to love one another, encourage one another, pray for one another, accept one another, bear one another's burdens, and build up one another. The only way you can obey these commands is in a small group! We really do need each other. God never meant for you to go it alone in the Christian life. If you are lonely, the answer to your problem is to join a group.

Prayer will become more meaningful to you. Many people are hesitant to pray in front of others, especially in a large church. In a small group of six to 12, group members learn to participate in prayer by having a conversation together with God. No one is pressured to pray, but as they become comfortable, they will be able to pray sentence prayers and join in. There are many promises in the Bible related to group prayer. In praying together with a few others, we are drawn together and we find answers to the needs in our lives.

You will be able to handle stress and pressure better. Small groups provide excellent support in times of crisis, change, and stress. You will have a sense of stability and security knowing there are people who really care for you and are committed to standing with you.

You will have a natural way to share Christ with unbelieving friends, relatives, and work associates. It may be that some of your friends who don't know the Lord wouldn't be caught dead in a church. They have preconceived ideas and just the thought makes them defensive. But those same people may be open to an invitation to a casual Bible discussion in a home or office setting. In a small group, your unbelieving friend can ask questions and express honest doubts without feeling "put on the spot". When your friend sees the love, warmth, and honesty of your group, it will make him more receptive to the Good News.

You will develop leadership skills you never knew you had! The Bible teaches that every believer is given certain talents or "gifts" to benefit others in the family of God. Unfortunately most Christians remain Sunday morning spectators all their lives because large group meetings are primarily "sit and listen" situations. As you share and participate in a relaxed small group setting, you will discover your confidence and assurance rising. This will help you in becoming a disciple maker and eventually you will have the opportunity to open your own small group.

You will be like the Christian in the Bible! The book of Acts is very clear about how God intends for his people to grow and have their needs met in the church. We will never be able to hire enough professional pastors to meet all the individual needs in our family. God never intended for it to be that way! Small groups are exactly how they met during New Testament times.

In Acts 2:42, 44, 46-7, we are told that "They devoted themselves to the apostle's teaching and to the fellowship, to the breaking of bread, and to prayer. All the believers were together ...and the Lord added to their number daily those who were being saved." And in Acts 5:42, the first Christians met, "Day after day, in the temple courts and from house to house they never stopped teaching and proclaiming the Good News that Jesus is the Christ" (Acts 5:42).

At New Life, we are excited about the incredible potential of the network of small groups we are building within our church. Small groups have these benefits that no believer can afford to pass up. People tend to go after what will benefit them. Show them the benefits of attending the group.

Pre-Encounter

A very important aspect of consolidating is the Pre-Encounter. The Pre-Encounter course is designed to provide the new believer with the opportunity to bond with a cell group mentor and begin establishing a foundation in the knowledge of God. The first purpose for the Pre-Encounter is *verification*. During the pre-encounter, we want to confirm that the new believer understands what it means the gospel message of salvation. Did they understand what they did when they let you know that they wanted to accept Jesus Christ as their savior? The second purpose is *information*. You want to share with the free pre-encounter booklet that provides them information regarding salvation, water baptism, and the baptism with the Holy Spirit. The third purpose is *preparation*. At the Pre-Encounter, we want to tell them what is going to happen at the Encounter Weekend. This is where you share what is going to take place at the Encounter and what they need to take with them. The last goal of the Pre-Encounter is *expectation*. This is where we stir up an incredible anticipation of what God can do for them and in them at the next Encounter Weekend. This is where we communicate that something great is going to happen. Have them write a letter of what they want Jesus to do for them.

Now that you know the goals of the Pre-Encounter, let us focus on the details of how to make it happen. Once a person receives Christ, you need to contact the new believer within 24 hours. This is not an optional strategy. If a new believer came to church on Sunday morning, the best time to call them is Sunday night. Why? Sunday evening is the best time to call most people because they are home. Even more important is the reality that a new believer needs our attention as soon as possible. It is like the birth of a new child; the sooner they are attended after birth, the greater the chance is that they will make it. Every time you call a new believer, your voice communicates to the new believer that he matters and has not been forgotten. Don't allow time to go by and let the enemy discourage the new disciple who has been entrusted unto you.

You also want to do a home visit within the first week. The purpose of this home visit is to once again reinforce the decision they have made to receive Christ. You are also trying to reach out to them so that they will stay connected. It is also to establish a working relationship with you as his or her disciple maker. During your first home visit you want to begin bonding with your new disciple. Take the time to get to know them and let them know you. Bring a word of encouragement from the Scriptures. If you don't know how to do this, contact your cell leader and he or she will be more than willing to guide you. You will also cover topics such as salvation, fellowshipping with God, the baptism of the Holy Spirit, and the Encounter Weekend as you meet with him or her.

The goal of the Pre-Encounter is for you as the cell group leader to prepare the new believer to go to the Encounter Weekend. Consolidation must be seen as a process and not just a meeting. It must be seen as relationship building and not a follow-up routine. We are not just seeking to teach the new believer, but to prepare him or her to bear fruit. Without the Pre-Encounter, the new disciple may get confused at the Encounter and may experience less of an impact spiritually. Preparation is the key to inspiration. It is essential that this step be not skipped.

Meeting one-on-one is the best way to Pre-Encounter someone. You may chose to meet in a home, park, restaurant, or any place where the new convert feels comfortable and is free from distractions. It is important to emphasize that you need to get the new believer consolidated as soon as possible. Just like a newborn baby, the first 72 hours are the most important. Special attention and care is required for that new baby in the Lord. Some of them need intensive care. Keep in mind that God did not call us to just get people to make a decision, but to make disciples. That is at the heart of the Great Commission. Jesus spent three and a half years making twelve disciples; shouldn't we be doing the same?

When you make a visit at the home, as addressed before in this chapter, seek to establish a relationship. The meeting may last 20-30 minutes. Ask to see if they have any prayer requests. You may choose to ask him or her about a prayer request that they wrote down on the Welcome Card. It is important that you as a disciple maker show genuine concern. Some cell group leaders will do an introduction and then set up another meeting to go over the Pre-Encounter booklet. It's important that it's conducted in an environment where the new believer feels comfortable. The ideal place is in their homes. Why? A home visit allows you to see the true condition and living environment of the new believer. It is a great opportunity for you to develop true compassion and prepare the new believer within the context of what is familiar to him or her.

Names of new believers are given to cell group leaders depending on how the new believer came to church. If a cell group member brought someone to church, it is the cell leader of that group member that will begin the consolidation. The fruit belongs to those that do the work. If a group member is bringing people to the church, it only follows that he/she should reap the fruit of their labor. There's also an element of trust at work. If a group member brings a friend to church, it is much easier for the new person to trust the group leader who brought them to church because a prior relationship, no matter how small, was already developed. Group members are taught to bring their guest to the welcome table and to make sure that the group leader's name is written on the welcome card so that person can be reconnected with the person that initially brought them to church. If a guest comes to the church on their own or is invited by someone who is not in a cell group, they may be allocated geographically or by needs. Allocating people by location is not the preferred method. The preferred method is actually for people to be placed based on existing relationships.

Let me give you an example on how the process of consolidation works. John came to the 11:45 a.m. service on his own. After he received an invitation to receive Jesus Christ as his Lord and Savior, John and others who have accepted the Lord are invited to go with cell group members to meet with a consolidator. During that time, the consolidator makes sure that John has understood what had just taken place when he accepted Jesus as his Lord and Savior. John is asked if he has any prayer requests. The welcome card is filled out. He is told that he will receive a welcome call within 24 hours. This card is passed on to a worker who verifies who lives nearest to John. The card is given to that cell group leader by the time the service is over. John receives a phone call the same evening, and by the end of the week he has received a visit. The cell group leader begins going over the Pre-Encounter booklet. During the visit he is invited to attend a cell group meeting. By the end of the week he is attending a cell group and possibly signed up for the Encounter.

One of the advantages of being in a small group is the easiness and feasibility of getting to know each other quickly. They know who brought whom and it is much easier to make connections. As a disciple maker, make sure that those you bring to church complete the welcome card correctly. That card is like a medical file that represents a soul and each of those souls must be followed up with. Experts tell us that if a guest comes to church for four weeks in a row they have a 75% chance of staying in that church. These experts also tell us that if a new believer gets to know seven to eight people in the church they have great chance of eventually becoming a church member. The beginning of the consolidation process allows for new believers to get to know people quickly in the church. This increases the chances that the new believer will feel connected to the church. That's why it is vital that new believers begin the consolidation process as soon as possible. As a disciple maker, you will begin to lose your effectiveness to reach the new believer you brought to church as each day passes by without connecting with him or her. You are accountable to God for contacting and having begun consolidation with the new believer. The leadership of the church trusts that you are correctly following the steps in consolidating the new believer.

Consolidation works if you work it. I have found that when people have said, "It doesn't work," it is because they have not done it the way it was supposed to be done. If a group leader makes all the phone calls assigned to them but does not visit until weeks later and lacks fruit and multiplication in his cell, it is no wonder why the cell leader does not see results..

The Encounter Weekend

We find in the Scriptures that before great men and woman embarked on a great mission for God, they had an encounter with God. It was a definite point in time when they had an experience with God. Some of the greatest encounters in the Bible are documented in Abraham (Genesis 12), Moses (Exodus 3), Joshua (Joshua 5-13-15), Isaiah (Isaiah 6:1-8), Paul (Acts 9: 3-7), Peter, James, and John (Matthew 17:2). Throughout church history, great men and women of God had encounters with God. These encounters served as the catalyst for effective ministry.

The Samaritan woman in John 4 had an Encounter with Jesus. And just like her, when you have an encounter with Jesus, He will deal with your pain (v.18). In those days, husbands divorced their wives, but wives did not divorce their husbands. The woman was "put away" five times. She was rejected and felt tremendous loss five times. The more she opened up to Jesus, the more she experienced Jesus. Just like the Samaritan woman, He will deal with your past. The way to Jesus is not holiness; the way to holiness is Jesus. She had a past, but Jesus gave a promise. After an encounter with Jesus, her past was used as a testimony of God's greatness. Just like the Samaritan woman, He will reveal his presence (v. 26) when a person has an encounter with Jesus. Notice, in John 4:26, he says to her, "I am here now."

The Encounter Weekend is the "transformation" component of the Consolidation process. It is a time of separation for spiritual preparation and the transformation of a disciple. It is the heart of Consolidation. The purpose of the Encounter Weekend is for new believers and church members to have an Encounter with God, others, and self.

Encounter Weekends are usually conducted in a retreat center, hotel, or any other place that is removed from the distractions of life. It is interesting to note that when God wanted the children of Israel to have a special communion moment with Him, he said, "…The Lord God of the Hebrews hath met with us: and now let us go, we beseech thee, three days' journey into the wilderness, that we may sacrifice to the Lord" (Exodus 3:16). When Jesus wanted to reveal His glory to three of his disciples, he "bringeth them up into a high mountain apart, and was transfigured before the…" (Matthew 17:1). Jesus himself understood the value of getting away from distractions, pressures, and stresses to rejuvenate His spirit and heart in the presence of his Father (Mark 1:35).

During the Encounter Weekend, people have an opportunity to deal with their secret sins, vices, dysfunctions, sour relationships, and just about anything that would stop them from becoming what God wants them to be. These Encounter Weekends have transformed our church. I have seen people who were nominal Christians catapulted into vibrant leadership as soul winners. It is an intense time when God's Spirit deals with stumbling blocks in our lives. It is not just a weekend when people are under powerful teaching. It is a weekend that will bring about tremendous impact upon a believer in Christ and even unbelievers. At an Encounter Weekend, you may come across people who thought they were saved that were not really saved. There are people who have shown remorse for their sins but have never truly repented for their sins and turned to Christ for true salvation. They may come to the Encounter Weekend with what I call "cultural Christianity" and walk out with real Christianity. It is a weekend where strong bondages are broken. It is a time where we immerse ourselves in the presence of God and surrender all. It is a time where we become desperate in seeking His face and where we have a memorable life-changing encounter with God.

A period and season of prayer and fasting must precede the Encounter Weekend. The disciple makers and the church attribute strong and powerful Encounter Weekends to times of fasting and prayer. At New Life we spend three days of fasting and prayer during the beginning of the week of the Encounter Weekend. As a disciple maker, let me encourage you to spend three days praying and fasting during a mealtime. Pray for each group member that you are taking to the Encounter Weekend. Also pray for the teachers and guides.

A disciple maker once told me, "When your leaders know the importance of the Encounter, your leaders will do even the impossible to make it." It is imperative that if you as a disciple maker bring someone to the Encounter that you attend as well. The Encounter is a prime time opportunity for the disciple maker and the new disciple to spend quality time with each other. It is also very meaningful for the disciple to know that their leader is there in this important weekend in their lives.

At the end of the Encounter, we return back to church for a testimonial and baptismal service. This is a great time for the new believer to invite their family and friends. You can use this opportunity to win their family and friends to the Lord. Before the Encounter, call family and friends of the new covert to come to this special Sunday service. This is a great opportunity to reach a new convert's family. With those family members and friends who accept the Lord at this event, you can start planning for them to attend the next Encounter Weekend.

Selection and Training of Leaders for the Encounter
Spiritual Guide

On every Encounter, there is one person who is assigned to be the spiritual guide. The senior pastor has the prerogative to be the spiritual guide or assign someone else to do it. What is the spiritual guide responsible for? The spiritual guide is responsible for all the spiritual aspects of the Encounter. This person is given the responsibility to select which teachers he will use in that particular Encounter. They check that the lessons being taught are on track with the mission and goal of the Encounter Weekend. He or she is the tone setter. The spiritual guide will come in and interject after a lesson, if needed.

Encounter Guides

The Encounter Guides are essential in making the Encounter a life changing experience.

It is a great privilege to be used of God as an Encounter Guide.
At the Encounter you have an opportunity as a leader to be a Guide. As a guide you will have the opportunity to minister in prayer, facilitate the small group sessions, spend time with participants during breaks and meals, reach out to isolated group members, and meet other needs as they arise. As a guide, you need

to be trustworthy. Confidentiality has to be upheld by every guide. People only share when they feel safe. Confidentiality creates an atmosphere of trust and openness. Having worked in the counseling field for many years, I can tell you that trustworthiness is essential for any type of meaningful change to occur.

Keep in mind that many people who attend the Encounter come with many hidden hurts, unfinished business, silent frustrations, deep bitterness, and scars. Just because a person has attended church for many years does not automatically mean that there are no hidden issues to be dealt with. I have yet to see an Encounter Weekend where one of the many topics has not touched one person or the other.

These issues best surface and expose themselves when people feel that they will not be judged for it. If there is information that is above your skill level as a guide, it should go to your leader or pastor.

As a guide, you need to have a prayer life. Throughout the weekend you should maintain an attitude of prayer. Gather them together for group prayer before sessions.

An Encounter Guide has the following responsibilities:

Before the Encounter Weekend

Do expect for God to use you. What you say, pray, and do at the Encounter can have a lasting impact in the life of someone who is in desperate need of a touch from God. You should come expecting that the Lord will use you as a vessel for His power and deliverance. Remember that without faith, it is impossible to please God. Whatever you are assigned to do at the Encounter, do it with anticipation that God will make an impact in someone's life through your obedience and service. A great missionary once said, "Expect Great Things From God, Attempt Great Things from God." Expectation is contagious. If you are excited for what God is going to do, so will others around you. This is why you want to keep a faithful attitude.

Pray and fast at least one meal a day for the first three days of the week before the Encounter Weekend. We want God to show up! It is the presence of God that brings the power of God. If God does not show up, then our investment in this three-day weekend will be for nothing. Many issues that people bring up at the Encounter retreat can be dealt with through God's Spirit. This is why it is imperative that the atmosphere for God's presence be created by leaders and disciple makers who intercede in prayer.

Do deal with your personal issues before going to the Encounter. Remember that you will be entrusted with people who are deeply hurting and in emotional pain. You want to come to the Encounter Weekend with a pure and clean heart. Seek to come with a heart free of pain and issues that may interfere with you ministering to someone in need. What you do in private will have an impact on the participants during the Encounter Weekend.

It is fine to feel nervous about ministering on the Encounter. Don't feel inadequate if you are new in your role as a guide. The main thing is to keep the main thing the main thing. Come with a willing heart to bless those at the Encounter. It is in our weakness that God shows up strong. The key is to surrender and yield to the Holy Spirit.

Do interact with those going to the Encounter at the church. Try not to isolate yourself from those who are attending the Encounter Weekend. They will have questions about their walk with their Lord. This is a great time to bond, especially with those who you brought to the Encounter who will be part of your cell group.

Be early. Be on time to each session. As a cell leader and disciple maker, you are a role model to those attending. If you are late, the people you brought will get a non-verbal message that says, "It is not important to be on time." You are communicating by arriving on time that this matters. It is very important that you are early at church before departure. In this manner, you can ease any fears or apprehensions that the new believers and first timers may have prior to leaving. Also, if you are bringing someone to the Encounter and they are running late, you are the contact person to let those in charge know about it. Once we arrive at the Encounter site it is important that you are there early for each session. You may be needed and we can only count on you if you are there.

Do welcome participants as they come in. You are an attitude setter. Your love and acceptance will help the new people feel like they belong and help eliminate any apprehension they may be experiencing. Take time to learn people's names. Greet the participants in a way that they feel glad to be there. For some new Christians, this is a brand new experience and it is very eventful time in their lives. Some may feel apprehensive, scared, or confused. A smile or a warm gesture can make a guest feel welcomed and wanted. You want to communicate love and acceptance, especially at the beginning.

Express great expectations for the weekend. Your words of expectation can become a seed of faith in the heart of those seeking for more of God. What you verbalize the new disciples will actualize. Negativity, complaints, or murmuring should never be heard by anyone in the Encounter coming forth from any leader or guide. As a Disciple maker, you need to make your "concerns go up, praises go down". This means that if you have a concern, it should never be heard by those we are ministering to. It is neither right nor fair to burden new believers with this load. If you do have a concern, bring it to the attention of your leader. They have the maturity and wisdom to handle it. As a helper in the Encounter, speak words of life and faith to the participants. Let them find hope through the level of expectation.

Be available to load equipment and luggage as needed. Making an Encounter Weekend happen requires the help of everyone in the leadership team. What you do or don't do matters. Ability without availability helps no one. We are always looking for ways to maximize the time during the Encounter. This occurs when everyone lends a hand, even with things that may not seem so "spiritual". But keep in mind that there is nothing more spiritual than serving someone else!

When arriving to the retreat center help in the escort of participants to the meeting place. This allows for order and organization to take place and for the first night session to begin on time. Rooms are assigned after the first session is over.

Do be friendly and express excitement for the first session. This first session is of utmost importance. It is the tone setter for the rest of the meeting. It has been said that it is the root that blesses the fruit. The first session is the root meeting that sets the foundation for the rest. This is why it is key that you share and express enthusiasm in the Lord for what he is going to do.

Luggage is taken to the rooms after the first session is over. Let the participants know that they need not worry to get their private belongings until after the first session is over. This allows us to start the meeting on time and focus on what they came for.

Always be available to deal with whatever is needed. If the problem comes to you, you own it. If it is too difficult for you to handle or you don't have the appropriate answer, then let your leader know. When you have a servant attitude and action, you are modeling Christ to them.

Look for those who have a greater need and are looking for someone to provide spiritual support throughout the weekend. Allow God to use you in ministering to someone in need. Not one leader or individual can address every need in the Encounter. Everyone has been blessed with a gift from God in order to serve others in the Encounter. Let God use you.

Facilitate small group discussion. You may be asked to run a small group discussion with the goal of allowing people to process their experience and what they are learning. If you are asked to run a small group at the Encounter, stay on topic. Do be a good listener and learn what to listen for. Help group members focus on themselves and not on others that are not present. The main question group members should be asking themselves is, "what do I need to change or have dealt with by God?" Do not allow anyone to monopolize the group's time. Do model transparency before group members. Do encourage confidentiality among group members.

Enforce a "lights out" rule. One of the biggest temptations during the Encounter is to stay up talking during nighttime. If participants do not get proper sleep, they will not be able to receive attentively what God has for them during the day. No discussions among roommates when lights are out. It is your responsibility to enforce this rule. If you don't enforce it, it disturbs and keeps others up. No one is to be outside of their rooms after lights are out. Staying up and talking about the Bible is not a justification for staying up. Bible-focused discussion will take place throughout the Encounter that is specifically focused on bringing healing and deliverance.

Be prompt for breakfast with your group. This will ensure that the morning session begins on time.

Pray for others. Be led by God's Spirit. Don't rush it. Do be sensitive to their needs. Do feel free to ask specifically what they need prayer for. Do be confidential if they share with you. Do be prepared spiritually before the sessions. Come early for a time of prayer during the morning devotionals.

When fatigue or tired, keep your attitude in check. The Encounter can be very physically demanding upon your body. It is easy when tired to allow ourselves to be impatient, ultra sensitive to what someone may say, or become angry quickly. If you need to vent, do it with those who are there to support you. Remember, concerns go up and praises go down. At no moment should a guide complain about anything to a participant. See the leaders who are in charge when a problem develops that you cannot handle or is causing you to lose focus. Avoid any form of gossip or backbiting.

If you see anyone not complying with the "complaints go and praises go down" principle, see a leader in charge.

Do encourage other guides. We need each other. We are one team and as a team we need to infuse courage and strength to our fellow co-workers in Christ.

Do not allow the enemy any kind of a foothold throughout the weekend. Be careful with your thought life. Dwell on the thoughts of God.

After the Encounter

Check the rooms for any items that anyone may have left behind. We want the Encounter to be a good experience to the very end. In the excitement to go to church and leave the retreat center or hotel, it is very easy to leave something behind. Be your brother's keeper.

Be open to opportunities to minister with people in your car on the way back home. Take time to ask those who went to the Encounter what the Lord did in their lives. It is a great way for the new believers to learn to share their testimonies. It is also a great source of encouragement for you to know that all the work you did was not in vain.

Thank God for having given you the opportunity to be used of the Lord. Always keep an attitude of gratitude. There is nothing like being used of the Lord. This is a great privilege that the Lord has granted you. Let the Lord know how grateful you are for it.

Objectives for the Encounter

You want to stay focused on the goals for the Encounter Weekend. I myself have attended numerous retreats in the 25 years I have been a Christian. Many of them included recreational activities of many sorts. Most of the retreats were mixed with "fun" activities and with Bible teachings and praying. The Encounter Weekend is a spiritual boot camp. There is no time for swimming and playing a baseball game. I am not against those types of camps. I love to have fun. But this is not what the Encounter Weekend is about.

Encountering the Encounter

The Encounter is a face-to-face meeting with God.

The ultimate goal of an Encounter is transformation. Transformation will only take place when they have an experience with God. Only a personal experience with Jesus produces a personal relationship with Jesus. In some traditional churches, the focus of a retreat is on events. The only problem is that events seldom produce a lasting passion and it is only when people have an experience with God that they will be transformed. We find biblical grounds for what occurs at the Encounter. Jacob first had a personal experience with God through separation. Before he had an encounter with God he separated himself from everything he had identified himself with: family, business, and friends. God requested from Moses and the children of Israel to be separated to a mountain to seek him for three days. We find him investing three days away from the natural to experience the supernatural. We also find that when Jacob had an encounter with the Lord there was a wrestling. At the Encounter people are confronted with themselves. What occurred at the end of Jacob's wrestling? God changed his walk forever. When people go to the Encounter Weekend, God wrestles with their inner fears, rejection, shame, sin, and guilt; they come out walking differently in their walk with the Lord. After an Encounter, they should never walk in life the same. Why? Their very nature is changed. When people truly have an encounter with God, they cannot be convinced out of it. The encounter weekend is a time and place where we create an environment for people to have an experience with God. We take people from the busyness of the world, away from its the noise and distractions to His presence.

The Encounter is won before the Weekend starts. If the people we take to the Encounter are to have an experience with God, we must set the spiritual stage before we even preach the very first message.

How? As we stated before, it begins through prayer and fasting. Pray that those who will be teaching will receive a fresh Word from God. Through prayer and fasting, we can believe God that those who will be sharing in Word will come with a prophetic proclamation that will speak directly unto the lives of those attending the Encounter. Preparation never allows an Encounter to be the same. An Encounter should never loose its freshness. Another aspect of preparation for the Encounter is the Pre-Encounter. As we mentioned before, the pre-encounter wets people's appetites to expect more from God at the Encounter. Please refer to the Pre-Encounter section for details.

The Encounter is an impartation.

It is about the multiplication of the anointing (Numbers 11). As a leader and disciple maker, you must first understand that the vision is not only an apostolic movement but also a prophetic movement. You must embrace the prophetic anointing promised by the Father in Joel 2:16.

There are two major impartations that take place at the Encounter. First there is an impartation of a Rhema Word. A Rhema Word is a specific word for a specific person about a specific area of their lives God is dealing with concerning those attending the Encounter. It is the word that touches the minds or the deepest part of their soul.

The Encounter prevents burn out in our ministry.
It groups the effort of all of the entire leadership team in one weekend to touch as many people as possible through the power of the Holy Spirit. It multiplies the effect of many people working on seeing others restored to God and their families.

The Encounter goes through a process.
The Encounter weekend is designed to help people to go through a process of restoration and transformation. Let us look at the five steps in the process.

Openness

One of the most important things people need to understand is that there will be no change in their lives unless they are open and sincere with God. There has to be total transparency. The Bible says that he who hides sin shall not prosper. This is why early in the Encounter Weekend, we emphasize the importance of becoming transparent with God and honest with themselves. When openness occurs, change can begin coming in.

Brokenness

Then we take the people to a place of deep repentance. They take responsibility for their own sins. Brokenness takes place when we have a revelation of what Christ did at the cross. The work of Christ on the cross is the key for the Encounter to have a lasting effect in someone's life. This is why is imperative that you pray that everyone attending the Encounter has a revelation of the cross in their lives. When brokenness occurs, reconciliation with God begins.

Inner Healing

People often want to be used of God, but can't because of past hurts and resentfulness. It is difficult to heal others when we are hurting in the inside. Healing from past hurts liberates new believers from the grip of bitterness and hatred. Often forgiveness becomes a central focus in this part of the process. When healing occurs, the restoration of relationships can transpire.

Deliverance

Many people come to the Encounter with habits, addictions, spiritual bondages, and strongholds in their personal lives. This is why we focus at the Encounter on spiritual warfare, bondage breaking, and strongholds being broken. We have seen countless people set free from drug addiction, alcoholism, promiscuity, gambling addictions, demonic influence, and other life controlling problems. When deliverance occurs, freedom comes in.

Vision

When God changes us, it is for a purpose. When God calls us out of darkness, He brings us into the light to do a work for Him. He gives us His vision. His vision is to win souls and make disciples. But to do His vision, we need power. This is why we introduce attendees at the Encounter to the Baptism of the Holy Spirit. They encountered the love of the Father, the Crucified Son and now the baptism of the Holy Spirit. Once they have received the power, they can go on with God's purpose and vision for their lives. Pray for each person you take to the Encounter to receive the Baptism of the Holy Spirit. When the vision is imparted, purpose can begin.

What is the result of this process? Fire. At the end of the Encounter, we want to see people ablaze for Jesus. We want to see them lit up for God. Only fire begets fire. So, when the people come out of the Encounter on fire for the Lord, they can set other people on fire for Jesus. This is exactly why you must go with the fire of the Holy Spirit to the Encounter: to pass on the fire of God in your life to others.

This is the reason why we refuse to modify the Encounter Weekend to include all kinds of activities that have nothing to do with having an encounter with God. Yes, there is plenty of time for deep fellowship and sharing, but it is at a different level.

Where does your enthusiasm as a cell leader and disciple maker comes from? This enthusiasm is born out of knowing what the Lord will do for your people as He transforms them through the process of openness, brokenness, inner healing, deliverance, and vision.

After the Encounter
Remember, you will be able to develop disciple makers and leaders to the degree that you are able to get people moving all the way to the School of Disciple Makers. If they don't move on, you will end up with no new potential disciple makers. This is why it is imperative that the people you bring to the Encounter immediately attend the Post Encounter class upon arriving church. We will talk later on in this chapter about the Post-Encounter, but

suffice to say that the continuation of their discipleship and growth in the Lord continues in the Post Encounter class.

At New Life, we allow those at the Encounter an opportunity to publicly declare their intentions to move on to the Post-Encounter during Saturday night. We even have a sign up sheet so that the Post-Encounter teacher and his/her small group leader can follow up in their intentions. We even go as far as inviting them to join the Post-Encounter 201 the very next morning. Why be so bold about it? We are mostly dealing with new believers. They need guidance and to be encouraged to move to the next level. Too often in churches, we wait too long before placing a believer in the training path of becoming a disciple maker. Another thing to keep in mind is that, believers need to be quickly edified through spiritual disciplines and learn how to deal with temptation.

Returning Home
We have a celebration service for those who attend the Encounter Weekend. This is normally done at the Sunday service after the Encounter. This is a great opportunity for those people you brought to the Encounter to ask for their family and friends to meet them at church for the testimony service. Family members and friends will hear life-changing testimonies from those who attended the Encounter. This service is beneficial for several reasons. First, it provides an opportunity for reconciliation to occur among family members. Often, men and woman will ask their family for forgiveness for wrongs done in the past. Husbands and wives will apologize to one another.

In one of our Encounters, we had a man who had been separated from his wife for seven years, openly apologize to his wife at the service for the way he acted in the past. They renewed their marriage vows to each other and openly shared their testimony to the church. This had a powerful effect upon his wife and the congregation. In essence, he was saying, "God Works!" And it moved others who have been sitting by the sidelines to sign up for the next Encounter Weekend. The excitement is so deep and genuine that it leaves an impact upon hearers in the midst of the congregation. It is one thing for the pastor to say how powerful and life-changing an Encounter Weekend was, but it is another thing for them to see the results with their very own eyes from a person that looks and sounds just like them. Your role as a disciple maker is to support and encourage the person you brought to the Encounter while they are sharing their testimony. If they need an extra support from you, don't be afraid to stand next to them while they are giving their testimony.

Second, the testimonies from participants open the door for the gospel to be presented to unbelieving family members or friends. It is a great evangelistic opportunity. Who can argue against the testimony of a loved one who has been changed by the power of God? We take a moment after the celebration and testimonies, to invite them to accept Christ as their Lord and Savior. This may be the last time some of them may ever visit the church. If a family member or friend accepts the Lord Jesus as their savior, feel free to accompany them to the front during the salvation call.

One Great Encounter
I have learned not to underestimate the value of an Encounter. Two thousand years ago, 120 disciples dedicated themselves to prayer and seeking the Lord. The result, as recorded in Acts 2, they had an Encounter with God. To this day, we are still feeling the impact of that great Encounter with God. Little did that group of believers know what kind of an impact they would have upon the world. Never underestimate the power and impact that the next Encounter will have upon the lives of those who you will bring.

Post Encounter

The Post Encounter is the third essential component of Consolidation. Once someone has attended the Encounter weekend, they proceed to join the Post-Encounter class. The Post Encounter is made up of two levels designed for the new believer to strengthen his walk with God. Level One focuses on the practical aspect of their walk with God. At New Life, we use a booklet named "Blueprint for Victory" that provides the blueprint for prayer, studying the word, stewardship, fellowship, dealing with temptation, and other pertinent subjects that will enable the new believer to develop a stronger walk with God. Level Two focuses on doctrine. They will learn the essential doctrines of Christianity and the strategy and structure of our church. Once a disciple completes the two levels, joins a cell group, and agrees to the New Life Membership Covenant, we welcome them to become an official member of New Life Outreach International.

But why not just allow people to just go directly to the School of Disciple Makers? New believers are often too green to go directly to the School of Disciple Makers, without first developing the spiritual disciplines in their lives. They must first learn to become a disciple, before they learn to make disciples. Remember, you want to develop a fruit that lasts. We must never become so eager to get people to open cell groups that we forget that ministry is built on character and solid disciples. Ministry is more fruitful when it is built on a solid walk with God. The Post Encounter serves as a catapult for the new believer to enter into the School of Disciple Makers.

The goal is to get 100% of the people who went to the Encounter to attend the Post Encounter. I can compare this to baseball. Baseball is a lot of fun. It is great when someone hits the ball and makes it to first base. But it is of no profit if a person stays in first base. The intention is to go to the next base, with the ultimate goal of making it to home plate. First base was <u>Winning</u> the new person to the Lord and second base was for new convert to be <u>Consolidated</u> (Pre-Encounter, Encounter, Post Encounter). Third base is the <u>School of Disciple Makers</u> and home plate is to <u>Send</u> them to open a cell group. The whole idea is to help them become a Grand Slam Disciple Maker. This will not occur, however, if they don't make it to second base – Consolidation. You as the Disciple Maker have the privilege in guiding and coaching the new believers and cell group members to make it all the way through the School of Disciple Makers. This should not be the responsibility of the Post Encounter teacher. Share with those you are helping enter the Post Encounter class the impact it had in your life and others. Testimonies are a great motivator at this point.

They need to hear from people who shared their same fears and apprehension in moving into preparation as a disciple. Many new believers struggle with inadequacies and insecurities. These issues need to be addressed during the Post Encounter.

Spiritual fathers are responsible and privileged to be fathers in the Lord. The only way for the next generation to reach their generation for Christ is for mentors to impart the vision, experience, wisdom, and skills God has given them. God wants to develop His kingdom not through those who work in isolation, but through those who work in cohabitation with their mentors. Mentorship is built upon divine order.

How to retain new people and guests

Just like a family gets itself ready for guests in their home, we must be ready as the family of God for the arrival and hospitable care of new guests. Jesus is our prime example of how to impact others. Jesus came to serve others. The best possible way to be a hospitable church is by serving our guests unselfishly. Our goal is for the guests to return and begin establishing relationships. Without healthy relationships, new guests will not be inclined to stay and they will eventually leave. Relationships are the glue that bonds new people to the rest of the church. Unfortunately, in many churches, people come in and then go out through the backdoors of the church. Let's take time now to understand the process on how to have guests return and then establish relationships at church.

First-time visitor

Guests usually make up their minds whether they will stay or never come back to a church within the first 15 minutes of the service. This is long before the pastor has preached a message. So it is crucial that we pay close attention in making first-time guests feel at home. There are four things we want to do for our guests when they first come in.

First we want to greet them. Everything we do at church should send a message to our guests that says, "You are welcome here and we are so happy that you joined us today." How you first greet a guest will determine whether they will come back or not. First-time guests tune in to the message you give out. Your smile, meaningful handshake, warm hug, or bright attitude communicate to our guests that they matter to us. Everything you do or don't do speaks loudly to the first-time visitor. Our facility also speaks loudly to our first-time guests. How our church facility looks also speaks volumes to our guests. If you see something you can immediately do to make the facility look presentable, do it, because it makes a difference. If you see a piece of paper in the floor, something out of place, or anything that needs tangible attention, go ahead and make the extra effort to make the house of God presentable to our first-time guests.

When you greet someone, greet him or her with a smile. Why? A smile communicates exactly what they are looking for, that is, acceptance. People are looking for love and acceptance. They want to know that they belong here. Make sure to smile and make eye contact. It communicates that you are sincere and real in connecting with them. The job of greeting is not just for ushers but also for everyone in the church. There is no substitute for love and acceptance. You can have the best sermons, worship, or special events, but without love and acceptance, people will feel unwelcome.

The next thing we want to do is to show them. First-time guests want to know what to do next as they walk in. If you see a first-time guest looking for the restrooms or standing as if trying to find where to go next, don't hesitate to direct them in a polite and caring manner. Feeling lost increases anxiety. Visiting a new church can cause anxiety all on its own. Do you remember the last time you got lost and someone showed you the way? There is only one word to describe it—relief.

The third thing we want to do for our first-time guests is to serve them. We want to provide five-star service to our first-time guests.

The difference between a one-star hotel versus a five-star hotel is in the details. Five-star hotels are attentive to every detail of service. How much more should we, who represent the Lord and his kingdom, attend to the detailed service of those who come to our church for the first time? When it comes to serving our first-time guests, always go the extra mile. If someone needs to know where the restroom is, don't simply give directions, but walk with them to the restroom. If someone wants to talk to a particular person, such as the youth pastor, take them with you and introduce them to the youth pastor. If the church is full in any given Sunday, why not give up your seat to a first-time guest? Treat and serve people as if Jesus came through the doors of our church for the first time.

Another key step is to connect with them. One of the tools we use is the Welcome Card. The Welcome Card is necessary, because it is the only way we can continue to stay connected with the guest. If you bring someone to church, always make sure they fill out the Welcome Card and turn it in to the ushers. Don't simply rely on the ushers to do this job. At our church, we work as a team and you are part of this team. As a newcomer, friends and family you bring to church trust you more than anyone else in the church. Encourage them to completely fill out the card and drop it in the offering basket. Keep in mind that it is through the Welcome Card that we begin the follow up process. On their way out of the church, they are also given a free gift.

The key to follow up is that you do it quickly, in a friendly way, and strategically. If you wait too long to implement this plan, you stand a greater chance of this person disconnecting. Don't be pushy but don't be passive either. Be friendly with an attitude that says, "I am here to be a blessing to you." Here are the steps you want to follow in the first 72 hours after someone comes to church for the first time:

If you were the one who brought the guest, introduce your guests to as many people as possible in church after service. Research shows that the more people they meet, the more likely they are to come back to church. Call them on Sunday evening and thank them for coming to church. Invite them to your cell group meeting. Also, encourage them to fill out the online survey, which asks feedback regarding the service. Keep in mind that most people don't work Sunday evening, so try not to miss calling them during this window of opportunity. Then send them a personal email and/or letter expressing how joyful you are they came to our church. The pastor will also be sending an email within the first 24 hours. The church will also be sending a letter mail within the first 72 hours (gift will be included).

Also, attempt to establish a time when you can go and do a home visit. Refer back to the section on home visits. Almost every guest that allows someone to come to their home for a home visit ends up coming back to church.

Second-time Visitor

The second-time guest is now more open and less apprehensive about being in church. They are more open to connect via relationships. The key to having second-time visitors come back is relationships. The best way for people to connect is in a small group. Small groups are more personable and conducive for people to get to know one another. If the second-time guest has not attended a cell group by now, ask them again to come to one of the meetings. The strategy for the second-time visitor is as follows. Call within the first 24 hours. Thank him/her again for coming back. Also, if there is a fun church-sponsored event (ex. picnic, basketball game, paintball, etc.) taking place in the near future, invite them. Fun events are non-threatening and enjoyable. People tend to connect quickly through these types of events. The pastor will send an email within the first 24 hours and a letter in the mail within the first 72 hours. Also, encourage them to attend your cell group and invite them to the next Encounter weekend. If they have not attended the Post Encounter class, take him/her with you to the class the following Sunday.

Chapter Four: Disciple by Teaching them

School of Disciple Makers

In the vision of the twelve, the goal is for every believer to become a disciple maker. Disciple making seldom happens by accident. It must come by design, preparation, and assimilation. Jesus gave the command for believers to make disciples. A disciple maker is by nature a leader. It requires leadership to make disciples. Jesus spent three years training the disciples to become disciple makers. We find Paul winning "about twelve men" and reasoned with them and others daily "in the school of Tyrannus" (Acts 19:7, 9). Two years later, we find that Asia Minor was under a tremendous move of God anfd multiplication of souls after the training these disciples received and were sent out. Jesus trained the few to reach the many.

He took his time in making sure that his twelve were trained to reach their generation through multiplication. There was no plan B. If they had failed in applying what he taught him in his school, the mission would have failed. The training of Jesus was focused on continuing his mission of seeking and saving the lost.

The School of Disciple Makers has five goals: (1) to impart a passion for souls, (2) to prepare the new disciples makers to conquer through prayer and intercession, (3) to provide training in the developing of a cell group, (4) teach students how to develop a team of twelve, (5) impart in the students the values of the cellular vision. The typical Bible institute or Bible college focuses primarily on increasing Bible knowledge. I know that the training that I received at my Bible college focused on increasing biblical knowledge and methods of studying the word of God. This is admirable and I am very grateful for the education I received during those four wonderful years. However, the School of Disciple Makers goes a step further. It focuses on how to implement the vision of Jesus in reaching this world. We often learn the "what" but lack the "how" of ministry.

For fourteen years as a Pastor, I struggled in finding how to make "church happen". Often, I would continually ask myself, "What is the best way to reach my community for Christ? Did I miss something in Bible College?" Many young and new pastors often come with the idea that if they teach homiletically correct sermons that their churches will soon be packed with people. I know because I was one of them. The fact is that there are thousands of great preachers with small churches. There is no strong correlation between just preaching great sermons and drawing masses of people into the church. I do believe that great preaching is one of the essential pillars in having a great and growing church, but other pillars are necessary in building God's temple. I know how it feels to have prepared what I considered a great sermon only to be discouraged after service and say to myself, "I wished more people would have heard this important message."

The School of Disciple Makers is more than having students memorize information or Bible facts. In America, we are hungry for information. Many believers are under the illusion that if they know a lot about the Bible they will automatically become spiritual giants. If that were so, why then are 85% of our churches in America declining or have reached a plateau in their growth when they are exposed to more biblical knowledge than ever before? The School of Disciple Makers focuses in making disciples who are going to be fruitful in reaching souls for God. The kingdom of God is not going to grow from people who just know, but from those who also do. The School of Disciple Makers is about developing better men and women through a better method of reaching souls. The end goal of the School of Disciple Makers is to develop disciples who will develop many other disciples through the principle of twelve.

How is the School of Disciple Makers set up?

The School of Disciple Makers is divided into three semesters. A new group of students start every semester. Once someone has completed the two levels of the Post Encounter, he can then join the new cycle in the School of Disciple Makers.

The School of Disciple Makers trimester is divided as follows:

Level One: Classes focus on the family and ministry. Each student is charged with the commission to add three new people to the cell group they are currently attending.

Level Two: Classes focus on the vision. Students are asked to open a cell group with at least three other people.

Level Three: Classes focus on consolidation and evangelism. Each student is encouraged to grow his team to at least 8 people.

The lessons are designed to be simple. There are no complicated theological terms or concepts. They are not trying to develop theologians but disciples. These classes are accompanied by life seminars that focus on character building. Keep in mind that most of the people who will be going through the School of Disciple Makers will be new in the things of God. We don't want to make the mistake of neglecting to lay a proper foundation in new believers.

In each of the trimesters, there is a reading assignment. For example, in the first trimester students are expected to read the "The Disciple Maker." Every effort is made to make students feel like they are attending a real school. If we water down the School of Disciple Makers, you will end up with less than prepared disciple makers who will later encounter frustration and discouragement.

Each of the three levels is structured so that by the end of the training they could potentially have a cell group of around 12. What I love about the set up of the School of Disciple Makers is that students learn by doing. It is an "on the job training" approach to learning leadership. In his book, "The Coming Church Revolution", Carl George, in answering the question, "How do people learn best?", has suggested that most people learn the most when presented with a problem. It is when students open their cell groups that the questions they ask begin to change from mere theoretical and hypothetical speculations to real life learning. I have found students are now learning out of necessity rather than novelty. They become more attentive to what is being taught, for they know that they are going to have to apply it. If you have not opened your cell group, don't wait until you have perfect conditions. The best condition is availability, not ability. It is when you are eager to learn and apply what you have learned. You don't have to be perfect to open a cell group. You don't have to know every there is to know about ministry. You learn best by doing it. You learn best by applying what has already been imparted to you. Students in the School of Disciple Makers are allowed to open a cell group by the second trimester.

Attendance is required in the School of Disciple Makers. The reason we ask for students to attend classes consistently is because they can't implement what they don't know. If a particular student is not disciplined enough to attend the School of Disciple Makers and come on time, what makes you believe that this person will be punctual when he or she opens their cell group? Just like in sports, a student will do whatever they practice. Normally, if a student misses more than two classes, they have to repeat the level. The only way to be excused from class is due to a job scheduling conflict or illness. In the case of a job conflict, the student may be allowed to purchase the lesson in DVD or do it online. The student is also responsible for completing the assignments in a timely fashion.

Other Nuts and Bolts

There are a few other things to keep in mind regarding the School of Disciple Makers. One of the things that you want to let your students know from the very beginning is that they must open a cell group before they graduate. No one graduates who have not opened a cell group. If one of the objectives of the School of Disciple Makers is to produce cell leaders, then it would only follow that one of the requirements of graduating from the school is to do what they were taught to do, that is, to open a cell group. Otherwise, you are going to have people go through the School of Disciple Makers just to learn and not to do. Disciple making is not just a position occupied but also an influence exercised.

I have learned that ministries do not grow by accident. Don't ever fall in the mental trap that you don't have the right people to do this type of a vision and complete a School of Disciple Makers. You will never have the right people until you take time to develop them. Disciple makers are made, not born. If we, as a church body, wait for the right people to suddenly show up and make things happen in your church, we will be waiting a long, long time!

What ever happened to discipleship?

I am totally convinced that a major problem with churches today is that we are producing many church members and few disciples. Most new converts do not make commit to making disciples because they have not been truly discipled by a disciple maker. My pastor and mentor, Victor Torres, always taught me that the danger of not making disciples is that the church falls into the danger of always having to come up with a new "hype" or event on a Sunday morning service. We have today a new generation of new believers that do not make their spiritual development a priority in their lives. Worship is seldom part of their weekly spiritual experience, they lack discernment on moral issues, evangelism is not practiced, and stewardship is neglected. Why? I believe that personal discipleship must be present as a primary task of the church. We only produce what we plan for. It is not a lack of programs that we suffer from but a lack of personal discipleship. It is easy to blame the new believers for their lack of spiritual development. Healthy growth has always been the responsibility of fathers and mothers. And, healthy spiritual growth has always been the responsibility of spiritual fathers and mothers. Most discipleship programs just focus on Bible knowledge, but Jesus' discipleship program focused on character development.

SEND

Opening a Cell Group

The success of a church is not measured by how many people you get in, but by how many people you send out to win this world. Church should be a place where people come with a problem and are sent with a purpose. Sending disciples out to open a cell group is essential in fulfilling the Great Commission.

Cell groups were at the very core of the New Testament church. We find that soon after the disciples had a Pentecostal Encounter the leadership mobilized the new believers to meet from house to house (Acts 2:46). Keep in mind that this occurred even prior to the persecution of Christians. Peter and other apostles made it a point to nurture believers in the context of home meetings (Acts 5:41-42). It was at Cornelius' house that a Gentile first received the word of God (Acts 10:22-24). It was at a home that believers were banding together in prayer for Peter to be released from jail (Acts 12:12). Paul's strategy in reaching Ephesus was to minister from house to house (Acts 20:20). There were house churches in the home of Aquila and Priscilla (Romans 16:3-5; I Cor. 16:19) and in Philemon's house (Philemon 2). Home cell groups were a way for believers to capture their homes for Christ. God's strategic plan has not changed. Cell groups are not a new fad. They are the restoration of the New Testament strategy to win this world for Christ.

The Mennonite church in Ethiopia had 5,000 members in 1982, when all its buildings were confiscated, its leaders imprisoned, and the people forbidden to meet together. As a result, the church went underground and met in cells in people's homes. Ten years later, in 1992, when the Communist government was overthrown and the church came out of hiding they had over 50,000 members! The same thing happened in China and approximately 30,000 people surrendered their lives to Jesus every day! Cells are the only solution to a church facing hostility. So whether we are facing an incoming harvest or hostility, we need cell groups to face it. We have not been called to survive, but to thrive. Jesus said, "The gates of hell will not prevail against the church" (Matthew 16:18).

He was not speaking in this scriptural passage of a church retreating from the enemy. He was referring to a church moving forward and the stronghold of Satan will not be able to stop it.

Cell groups are not just another innovative program among other programs in the church. It is the very heart and soul of how we are to do the Great Commission and Great Commandment. It is the smallest common denominator unit of the church. The biggest churches in the world operate as cell churches. It is the best context to breed leaders and disciples who will make disciples. This is why cell groups must become the central focus of how we go about fulfilling the Great Commandment and Great Commission (Matthew 26:36-38, 28:18-19). Why? Because Christianity can be summed up in one word: relationships. And relationships are best developed and forged in small groups. We need to see cell groups having church on Sunday instead of churches just having cell groups. Today, we have many people who don't want to just believe, they want to belong. One of the major problems that are occurring in churches without cell groups is that people may start to feel like they are just another face in the crowd on Sundays. Cell groups allow them to feel connected in a meaningful way. If cell groups are not operating effectively and efficiently in our church we will lose a large portion of the harvest, or at best we will only poorly contain it. Only cell groups can provide the practical training ground and apprenticeship that is needed to equip disciple makers.

A common question asked by students in the School of Disciple Makers is, "How do I go about opening my cell group?" Focus on a few and then expand. Develop a core of three or four men or women, who will serve as role models to the rest of those who will be joining later in the group. Jesus seemed to have followed this pattern when he first focused on John, Peter and James. Of course, you want to reach as many people as possible, but never lose the personal touch in ministering to the people you are reaching.

Mentoring takes time and effort. The job of the new cell leaders is to begin to invest and pour out his life upon these core group members. This includes getting involved in the families of these

94

group members. Jesus did it in order to remove any distractions or stumbling blocks (Matthew 8:16). Jesus reached Peter, then his family to reach the community. Building a cell group takes time because meaningful relationships take time. It is one thing to have 12 people in a cell group, and, it is another thing to have 12 fully developed disciples.

Your group members should not be a part of another cell group. If you allow someone to be in multiple cell groups, sooner or later the disciple will find himself in a conflicting situation of having to answer to two different cell leaders. For example, if cell group leader named "Mary" and another cell group leader named "Janice" were to ask that particular group member to attend their evangelistic event, whom will they go to? Also, once this cell group member becomes a cell leader, whose G12 will they attend?

This also brings up the issue of whether or not you should have people from other churches in your cell group. When making disciples, it is unproductive to have someone who is part of another church in one of your cell groups, unless the person is looking for another church. First, the members from the other church should be receiving discipleship from their church. They should be spending their time and energy building their church and following the vision God has given to their pastor. The other issue pertains to your time and energy. Keep in mind that as a cell leader, you are attempting to build a team of 12 leaders. If you are spending all of your time with people who are not going to be ultimately committed to the development of your team, you will never be able to multiply. You may have a large group of people, made up of people from different churches, but that is all that you will have. You will not be able to develop your G12, which will stop you from building your G144 and so on. We normally give people who attend other churches 4 to 5 weeks to decide if our church is what they are looking for.

A Cell Group Meeting Format

There are various ways of running a cell group meeting. The following is a sample on how to schedule an open cell group meeting:

Welcoming: Welcome your guests with love and acceptance. Be friendly (Proverbs 18:24) and make the first move as the leader to make the guest feel at home. Don't wait for the guest to introduce himself. Listen with your total undivided attention. Honor the time your guests are spending with you by starting on time. Always start on time! You reward those who come on time when you start on time. Learn their names as soon as possible. Everyone likes the sound of his name. If they present you with a problem, show them concern for their situation.

Opening Prayer: Allow for others in the group to open in prayer. Always compliment someone after finishing opening in prayer, especially if he or she is a new Christian.

Worship: If no one in the group plays an instrument, use a CD or an MP3 player for worship. Limit the worship section to a maximum of two songs.

Vision Casting: Go over the vision each week. You may also take a moment to deal with group logistical issues, such as childcare assignment and goal setting, for the meeting next week. The goals are to have four guests per month, three to the Encounter Weekend, two to the School of Leadership, and two to be send out as group leaders per month.

Group Discussion/Teaching: You want to make sure that everyone gets to participate in the discussion. People are more likely to change if they are given an opportunity to share. Allow for interaction and avoid talking down to group members. Make it safe for anyone to share. The more secure they feel, they more likely they are to share deep issues. Don't allow interruption or anyone to monopolize the group time. Don't allow group members to deviate from the topic. Your cell leader gives the topic of the week to you. This way, every cell group teaches the same lesson for the week and the church moves as one.

Prayer Request: Encourage group members to share their needs and to pray out loud their prayer request. If you have a large group, you may want to divide them into small groups of four each. Take time to introduce the Prayer for Three.

Offering: Offerings are collected during cell group meetings. Assign a trustworthy believer who will serve as a treasurer and collects the offering. The offering is to be brought by the cell group leader to his cell group leader until it reaches the primary G12 meeting. You should discourage group members borrowing monies from each other or the promotion of personal business in the group.

Testimonies: You want to give an opportunity for people to share personal testimonies. It is a faith booster and people get to see, in a tangible way, how God answers prayer. A testimony allows you to finish the meeting in a high positive note.

Close in prayer: Close in prayer and send everyone with a blessing.

TIME: I meet with my G12 once a week. You may choose any time of the week or weekend, as long it not during a Sunday service. Most cell meetings take place during the evening. Just keep in mind that whichever evening you choose, your group members will not be able to have their cell group meeting that evening. Only your future G144 will be able to have a cell group during the same time you are having your G12 group.

LOCATION: It is preferable that meetings take place in a home. In the inner city where apartments may be small and lacking a backyard, it may be conducive to have some of the cell groups in the church. However, the preferred mode is to conduct the cell meetings in people's homes. Once we get to the point in the meeting where we need to divide homogenously, we go into separate rooms.

Be open to the operation of the gifts of the Spirit. There are things going on in people's lives that are obvious from the outside. At times, you may find God giving you insight into someone situation. If there is one gift I do ask the Lord to use me in it is the gift of prophecy. A prophetic word edifies, strengthens, and encourages leaders to continue in the work of ministry. Remember, many of your leaders will experience seasons of discouragements and disappointments. Most veterans in the G12 vision will place a heavy emphasis on the prophetic. The word "prophetic" means many things to many people. Some have misused its use in the church and small groups. But we ought not to throw out the baby with the bathwater. The Bible is very clear as to its value and validity in the church and small groups (I Corinthians 14).

A word about the cell leader and prayer

Leonard Ravenhill once said, "Revival delays because prayer decays." Prayer is the oil that lubricates the vision of a cell leader. Samuel Chadwick spoke of prayer this way, "Prayer is the acid test of devotion." Prayer starts revival and cell groups contain revival. A cell group leader must be committed to pray at least an hour a day. If you have not established a prayer life, start with 5 minutes and then work yourself up to an hour.

If there is no prayer, there will be no power. It is in the place of prayer that we see the Father's vision: multiplication and transformation. It is in prayer that we become vessel by which the Holy Spirit will bring the vision of the Father to pass. Prayer is no substitute for work, but neither is work a substitute for prayer. Make it a point to pray for each of your group members daily and fast a meal in the day of the cell group meeting.

In John 15:16, Jesus tells us that "you would go, and bear fruit, and that your fruit would remain, so that whatever you ask of the

Father in My name He may give it to you." Jesus is setting a condition for prayers to be answered. He is saying in essence, "if you make it your business to go and win souls and keep them, I will answer your prayers." Why? It is because you are doing the Father's kingdom business. You are following God's agenda here on Earth. It is what Jesus was referring to when he said, "Seek ye first the kingdom of God and all of these things shall be added to you."

We need to pray the vision. We catch the vision by praying the vision. In John 17, Jesus prays out loud for the disciples to hear his intimate moment with the Father. This is the longest recorded prayer of Jesus in the Bible. It focuses on the twelve. If you want to hear what is really important to someone, listen to his prayers. We get to listen to the heartbeat of Jesus in this prayer. His main concern was his twelve. Jesus won them, consolidated them, discipled them through the Word and sent them out into the world. If Jesus' prayer was focused on the twelve, and he is the Master Teacher, should not we, as his students, pray for our twelve as well? You may say, "I don't have twelve people to disciple now." Jesus prayed all night to select his twelve (Luke 6:12-13). It is one of the few times recorded in scriptures where Jesus is found praying all night, and it was in regards to selecting his twelve. The quickest way to get a passion for making a team of twelve disciples is to pray about it. You will not get the heart of Jesus until you know the heart of Jesus. And you will not get to know the heart of Jesus until you spend time with Jesus.

Developing a Group of Twelve Leaders

The number twelve has special significance in the bible. It is the number that signifies and represents perfect government. We find in the Old Testament that there were twelve tribes (Ex. 28:21), twelve leaders who were sent to spy out the Promised Land (Josh. 4:1-10), and David had one general for each of the twelve tribes of Israel (I Chron. 29:6). Solomon had twelve princes who operated as chiefs (I Kings 4:7). In the New Testament we find that Jesus chose twelve men (Mark 3:13-19) to be his disciples.

Jesus was a strategist. His methods were flawless and the results are still been felt today. What made Jesus' model of ministry so effective? In the average church, most discussion and conflicts revolve not around what we believe, but how we do church. Most pastors and church member when asked, "Do you believe that the Great Commission is still relevant for the church today?" They will be quick to answer with a resounding, "Yes!" But if you were to ask them, "How would you go about accomplishing this task?" you will get many different answers. Most would point to church programs and activities. But the real question should be, "How would Jesus go about reaching the masses today?" I believe that the answer would be, just like he did when he walked this Earth. He did it through a group of twelve men.

Notice that Jesus' strategy was not to spend most of his time with the masses but with a selected twelve. These twelve would probably have been rejected at a Bible college or seminary. They were ordinary men living ordinary lives. From the outside, they did not seem like the type of men who would turn the world upside down.

Why did Jesus select twelve? As mentioned before, the number 12 represents divine government. Jesus gave us a model of the best way to reach the multitudes. When he saw the multitudes distraught, he was moved with deep compassion (Matthew 9:35-37). He selected and called the twelve to meet the needs of the people (Matthew 10). It is interesting to note that there were about 120 disciples in the upper room when Pentecost took place (Acts 2), which is divisible by 12. The point is that when God wanted to build a nation of believers he did it through the principle of twelve. It is not a matter of finding something mystical about the number twelve. But, its effectiveness in accomplishing God's objectives for this world is consistently evident.

The great revivalist and founder of the Methodist church, John Wesley, understood the power of discipling new believers through small groups. He organized his followers into small groups. A Methodist society included all the Methodists in an area. It was

100

divided into groups, or classes, of 12. The people met each week to study the Bible, pray, and to share the status of their spiritual walk. Each class had a leader who reported to the preacher in charge of the society. Wesley provided his leaders a list questions for members examine themselves: "What known sins have you committed since our last meeting? What temptations have you overcome? How did God deliver you? What have you thought, said, or done that might be sinful? When the questions revealed sin, the offenders were given another chance. "If they forsook their sins," Wesley said, "wc received them gladly; if they obstinately persisted therein (in sin), it was openly declared that they were not of us. The rest mourned and prayed for them, and yet rejoiced, that, as far as in us lay, the scandal was rolled away from the society. Because the leaders knew each class member intimately, they could tailor their words to each individual need." He understood that without cell groups, all he had worked for would be lost. A 1763 trip to Wales caused him to give this advice to future Methodist generations: "I was more convinced than ever, that the preaching like an Apostle, without joining together those that are awakened, and training them up in the ways of God is only begetting children for the murderer. How much preaching has there been for these 20 years all over Pembrokeshire! But no regular societies, no discipline, no order or connection; and the consequence is that nine in ten of the once-awakened are now faster asleep than ever."

Charles Edward White. Copyright © 2001 by the author or Christianity Today International/Christian History magazine. Click here for reprint information on Christian History. *Issue 69, Winter 2001, Vol. XX, No. 1, Page 28*

How does the model work?

Pastor Cesar Castellanos received and implemented the principle of the twelve as a working model to reach cities, nations and continents. In his classic book, "Dream and You Will Win This World", he describes his discovery in this matter: "The Lord specifically told me, 'You will reproduce the vision that I have given you in twelve men and they should do the same with another twelve, and those in turn should do the same with still another twelve." In a recent articles he details it, "If I trained 12 people, reproducing in them the character of Christ in me, and each of them did the same with another 12, the continuation of this process, with every group of 12 transferring what they receive, would lead to unprecedented growth in the church." He is not kidding; he now has over 250,000 people in his church and still growing by over 10,000 per month! The good news is that this is not an anomaly. Churches all over the world and in the United States are reporting unprecedented growth in countries where church growth was declining.

The goal of a cell leader is to develop twelve disciples who will each open a cell group at a different time. Then each of those twelve leaders goes out and develops twelve leaders each. And the process continues on and on. Once the pastor develops twelve disciple makers who have opened, we call that group a G12. A true G12 is a group of twelve disciple makers. Once each of those twelve leaders develops twelve leaders each, then you have a G144. To the process goes a follows:

G-12
G-144
G-1728
G-20,736

The beauty in this process is that cells are not divided, but rather they multiply. In the traditional cell group model, once a cell group reaches a certain size, the group had to divide into two groups. The problem with this model is that once group member grew accustomed to each other, they often sabotage or resist any efforts in splitting the group. This feeling is understandable. Asking people to invest into something that later on will be taken away from them can be painful and discouraging. A pastor friend of mine recently told me that it took him three months to motivate a cell group in his church to split into two. In the principle of the twelve, church members never have to be split from one another into two separate groups.

In any given time the cell group leader runs his meeting and on at a different time cell group members open up their own cell groups. This way, the cell group members who eventually become leaders never have to leave the cell group. Once twelve cell group members become leaders, this group become a group of only leaders. The nature of their meetings will change. These meetings become primarily a time for deep mentorship and training. Keep in mind that a cell leader will always attend a cell meeting where he leads and in another time he is on the receiving end. So in one group he receives and in another group he gives. In one group he is being discipled, and in another group he is making disciples. In the old traditional model, weekly mentorship was not guaranteed. Many new cell leaders embarked in opening a cell, only to find themselves burned out and discouraged later on. The ongoing support was often lacking, unless a tight supervised system was in place.

Supervision and mentorship is set up to occur on a weekly basis. There are a couple of ways you can go about accomplish this. As group leaders, you may begin attending two meetings. One with your group leader, another time you meet with your multiplication group.

How Jesus got His twelve

Jesus built His team one person at a time. Jesus built his team literally winning one person at a time. The key is to be consistent in winning, consolidating, discipling, and sending new disciples. This is the way Jesus did it. He took about a year reaching out and bringing in the harvest. Don't be discouraged if you only start with a few. Everything great had a small beginning. Here is the good news: everyone you disciple from here on is more than what you had when you first accepted Jesus as Lord.

Jesus built his team after much prayer (Luke 6:12)

The Bible says, "It was at this time that He went off to the mountain to pray, and He spent the whole night in prayer to God. And when day came, He called His disciples to Him and chose twelve men, whom He also named as apostles." Why such dedication in prayer in selecting the twelve? It is because these men were going to serve as pillars in building God's house. Through prayer, God will impress upon your heart to select certain men and woman who will follow you as you follow Jesus. You don't want to leave the selection of your twelve to mere chance. You want a divine choice in the matter. It may save you hours of aggravation and seasons of pain. When it is God, you will be surrounded with men and women who, for the most part, will be faithful, available, and teachable to you and the Lord.

Jesus took about a year to complete his team

It amazes me that Jesus took around a year to select his team. Why? Because relationships take time to develop. You may find yourself with only half of the team months after you began to implement the vision. This ought not to discourage you. As you develop men and women of excellence into leadership, your ministry will become a magnet to other future leaders. Sometimes we get so excited about the vision that we want everything to happen all at the same time. You can have it all, but like building a high-rise building, you must build one level at a time. Building anything valuable, durable, and strong takes time. Remember that you are building a mentorship relationship that will probably last your lifetime.

Jesus showed them their future if they followed him (Mark 1:17)

What impresses me about Jesus is how He imparted vision to those around him. Notice how He showed them what He would make out of them when He said, "Do not fear, from now on you will be catching men." He first addressed their inadequacies; in this case, fear. Most people are afraid to enter into making disciples because of fear. Some put brakes on God in making disciples because of their inner fears and internal debate. They know that the vision makes sense and it works. But fears kick inside of them and say, "Can I really do this?" and "Will people follow me into this vision?" They may also think, "What if I start and I fail?" or "I don't have the skills and abilities." The fact is that Jesus faced the same concerns and possibilities of failure that you currently face. If you have fears to overcome, so will those new disciples who will be introduced to this vision. Talk to your leader about these concerns. If you don't talk about these fears, insecurities, and feelings of inadequacies, sooner or later they will become hidden agendas or a stronghold. Some of my initial leaders wondered whether they were capable of doing this vision. My wife and I spend many hours discussing fears with those who initially feared. Now they are among the most fruitful. Address these concerns and do not ignore them. I have seen disciple makers with good intentions bulldoze through the vision without taking the necessary time to address these concerns among the new disciples. These fears will surface sooner or later and manifest itself as resistance to the vision. It is not that they are necessarily resistant to you as a cell leader, but that they are protecting themselves due to the fears that have not been directly addressed.

Fear has an interesting anatomy. Fear comes from speculation. Speculation occurs when we begin to say, "What if it doesn't work?" Speculation always says, "What if...?" Speculation comes from uncertainty. Uncertainty comes from a lack of control. Fear is a failure to see that God is in total control of the situation you are facing. Fear is a failure to comprehend that God is always in complete control. You fear when you fail to relinquish control to God. This is why anxious people are control freaks! Fear will paralyze your faith dead in its track. Faith and fear are the antithesis of each other; they cannot cohabitate. When one starts, the other finishes. When one grows the other one dies. Faith is the end of fear. They both have its set of language, expression and manifestation. The problem with fear is that it breeds self-doubt. If lack of control is the genesis of fear, then God's greatness is the genesis of faith. Show your people how God wants to work his greatness through them. Speak to your leaders and people about the vision with faith, expectation and anticipation. Always speak with faith and solid hope about what the Lord is going to do. If you speak fear, you will only increase fear in them.

Not only did Jesus address their inadequacies, but He also showed them their future. Impartation of vision and commission is essential in this disciple making vision. He told them, "Follow me and I will make you fishers of men." That is what you should be saying, "Come under my leadership, and I will show you how to make disciples like you have never seen before." I know that we live in a church culture that says, "Don't look at me, look at Jesus." But recalled what Paul said to those he was mentoring in Corinth, "Be imitators of me, just like I also am of Christ" (I Corinthians 11:1). The word "imitators" literally means, "mimic." Why? Paul was mimicking Christ. Let them see in you the Christ-like leadership faith, positive attitude, values, and skills demonstrated before them. They will do what you will do. And they will believe if you believe. Speak life and expectation that God will certainly use them.

Jesus' words were so powerful that some brought others (John 1:40-42)

You will attract those who believe you have something valuable to say. Notice how Andrew brought his brother Simon Peter to Jesus to hear what Jesus had to say. Soon after, we find Phillip bringing Nathaniel to Jesus (v.45). Look for those who enjoy listening to you and are willing to receive the good, the bad, and the ugly from you. Look for those who are so excited to hear what God has imparted upon your heart that they enjoy bringing others to hear what you have to say. The best way to discern as to whether someone really flows with you is to see who loves to bring others to the house of God to hear what you have to say. This is why it is important that you continue staying sharp in the Word by attending the Bible Institute and reading good books.

Gift versus Earning Leadership

Gifts are given, but leadership is earned. God has given every believer different gifts to accomplish the work of God in winning souls and making disciples. However, leadership is something you earn. Let's look through a few biblical examples of this principle. Saul was given a gift from God to do the will of God. He had a calling. He had an anointing and he had received impartation from Samuel, one of the greatest prophets Israel had ever known. Samuel was a mentor and Saul was under his prophetic anointing. David was also given a gift. He had the same calling to leadership. He had the same anointing. He had received the same impartation from Samuel. He was mentor under the same prophetic anointing as Saul. They both had the same gift of leadership, so what was the difference between David and Saul? Why did the people want to follow David and not Saul?

The leadership that was honored by God and the people was the one who conquered giants. David earned his leadership by becoming a conqueror. A title alone does not make you a leader that people want to follow. People follow conquerors. The principle that leadership is earned is found also in the story of Deborah and Barak (Judges 4:9). It was Deborah who truly conquered and was honored as a leader. We also find this same principle at work in the story of Joshua and Caleb. Joshua and Caleb responded but the other ten of Moses' twelve forfeited their inheritance because they did not earn their leadership. They all had the same challenge: to conquer. I like what John Maxwell has to say about this: "There is a difference between like-minded leadership and the good old boy mentality." The "good old boy" mentality and leadership pampers, promotes, and protects those who are in, regardless of productivity. People honor fruitful leaders and leaders who multiply are honored by people. Disciple makers who show fruit and multiplication receive honor from those who follow. This is why at New Life, we don't give titles away just because someone speaks or sounds good. Titles follow those who have good fruit. So the question is not whether you potentially have an anointing or not for leadership, but whether you will work and bear fruit. When a twelve earns leadership, none will be able to say, "He or she did not earn their leadership standing in the G12." Why? It is because leaders are known by their fruit.

In 1 Chronicles 11:11, we see David making a call for conquerors. In verse 11, the Bible says, "Now David had said, "Whosoever strikes down a Jebusite first shall be chief and commander."
David gave them a challenge for leadership. He was saying, "You have to earn it and it is up to you." In 2 Samuel 23, we find a list of those who made his leadership team. I call it the wall and halls of leaders. Included in this chapter are all of David's G12 mentioned in 1 Chronicles 27. He also had "the three" and the "three of the thirty." These were mighty leaders. How did they make it into this special leadership team? They earned it. The common denominator among all of these leaders is that they all conquered. Josheb-bashebeth (also known as Jashobeam) became a mighty leader "because" (v.8) he conquered 800 men. Eleazar (v.9) fought when others fled. Abishai (v.18) fought 300 men with a spear and "he was most honored of the thirty, therefore he became their commander, however, he did not attain to the three" (v.19). Benaiah (v.20) defeated two Moabite warriors, a lion and 7.5 feet tall Egyptian with a club. Now God has called us in this generation, not to conquer land or territories, but to conquer the heart of men and women for God.

The question now becomes, what type of character do I build in my cell members so they can become twelve disciple makers who will change the world?

The Seven Qualities You Want to Build in Your Disciples

The first trait to build is consistency. Consistency is what we find as the trait that differentiated some of these mighty men from the rest of the men of Israel. We are told that Eleazer (v.9) and Shammah (v.11) stood their ground when others ran. David learned that despite the challenge, they were consistent. This is why Paul also told Timothy to entrust what he had learned to faithful men. Develop people who will not only start strong, but finish strong. A quitter will never see success in ministry. Those who are faithful are faithful because they don't stop believing. Those who believe conceive faithfulness. The day your cell members stop believing, is the day they will stop being consistent. This is why you want to continue speaking into their lives and encouraging their faith with God's Word. The reason why God granted the victory to these men was because they believed that they could win and conquer. We are told in Hebrews 11:33 that "...by faith conquered kingdoms..." A bad thought and seed came into the minds of the men of Israel and they began to say, "We can't," "It is too difficult and impossible," and "Why even try?" It is amazing how a wrong thought can rob a potential twelve of their destiny.

Consistent disciples say, "I am in." These are not excuse makers. Excuses are voices rooted in a lie that affects our faith and faithfulness to do the calling of God. Take time to deal with arguments and excuses your disciples may have. If they don't follow, you can't make them into disciples. This is why Jesus said, "Follow me and I will make you fishers of men."

The second trait is intensity. Someone can be consistent but not intense. Someone can be consistently and faithfully lame! Notice how one of David's men fought. The Bible says, "His hand ... clung to the sword." That is what I call intensity. It is very possible to go through the vision but not allow the vision to go through you. Someone may just go through the motions without intensity. Look for men and women like Eleazar; he fought with his heart. Where does intensity come from? Intensity comes from integrity. In other words, intensity is born of integrity because of conviction. Conviction is when you have strong beliefs that you are willing to die for. Only those who have convictions have intensity. Teach your men and women to have strong convictions. The calling of Christ requires a 100% commitment and surrender of all you are. A person with conviction says, "It is all about Jesus." A person with conviction says, "The church is the hope of the world and the only institution that lasts forever." A person with conviction says, "I will serve Christ by serving others." A person of conviction says, "Everyone needs Jesus." This type of person is unstoppable. Here is the good news: whenever you develop a person so that he or she has integrity and conviction, he or she will demonstrate self-initiative. You won't have to be after them all the time to do something for God. Intensity will lead you to initiate. Show me a person who does not take initiative and I will show you somebody who does not have intensity. We are told in verse 10 that "he arose." Develop people in your cell group who want to arise with intensity. Intensity will cause your cell members to arise out of the comfort zone. Intense people do not stand around to see if others are doing the right thing or not in order for them to get started.

The third trait is urgency. In all these stories of battle I find men who understand the urgency of the situation. It was not panic, but a passionate purpose. Something becomes urgent when it becomes a priority. If you want to develop people who are urgent about the reality that souls are going to hell without hope, then develop people with biblical priorities. This is why Jesus often called the disciples to evaluate their priorities. He understood that disciples without their priorities straight would not sense create a sense of urgency in their spirit.

The fourth trait is strategy. In 2 Samuel 23:16 says, "so the three mighty men broke through the camp." The key to their success is that they implemented a strategy. Teach your men the strategies on how to win, consolidate, disciple, and send. The more they know about how to do these things, the less fearful and insecure they will feel about making disciples. Often, people don't

110

do the work of God, not for lack of desire, but because they feel incompetent. Once a person knows how to do something, they feel less fearful about doing it. Your twelve are going to need the skills to become the kind of disciple makers you want them to become. Give them books to read and audio files to listen to. Show them strategies by modeling for them different ways to win, consolidate, disciple, and send. Many things your disciples will learn will not just be taught, they will learn by imitating you.

The fifth trait is harmony. For strategy to work you must have people who buy into the strategy. And to do this, you want to develop a team that has the same purpose and vision; they need to be in harmony. The key to harmony is agreement. Amos 3:3 "Can two walk together, except they be agreed?" harmony is a meeting of the minds. You need to say clearly what you expect. You will never have your twelve move as one unless they are in agreement with the vision. You need to model harmony by avoiding any type of gossip and slander. Slander is like a grenade. Those who slander do it openly and others quickly take notice. A gossiper is like a sniper. They shoot with their words and assassinate someone's character without the victim even knowing it. You need to develop the power of one. There is no substitute for oneness. It is going to require a team effort to break into the territory God has for you. Notice how you will not find in this passage any evidence of disharmony. There were not envious or jealous of one another. There was no unnatural competition at all to be noted. Just like harmony in music, where different people with different talents sing as one, so in ministry you want to develop a team who will use their different talents and gifts as one team. Keep in mind, your disciples will act just like you do. If you speak negatively against your pastors and leaders, your disciples will learn to speak negatively towards you. If you hold resentfulness and bitterness toward your pastors and leaders, you disciples will do the same. The old adage is always true; the apple does not fall far from the tree!

The sixth trait is bravery. These conquerors had a challenge inside of them. They confronted the fear of failure face to face.

Bravery is not the absence of fear but the conquering of fear. Teach your men and women to break strongholds. A stronghold is a wall of words that you believe to be true. It is what we call an argument. An argument is voice that speaks inside of you, which is rooted in a lie. It is something that has a strong hold on you. It only takes one stronghold and argument to cripple someone's bravery and courage. Strongholds can become familiar; we can get used to having them in our lives. We begin to excuse our limitations when an argument begins to take root in our minds. This is why we need to identify them and recognize they are not of God. What is wearing your disciples down? What weight have they accumulated in their hearts that makes them tired? What frustrates them? What thoughts make them give in and slow down? Whatever is repeating itself again and again, whether fear, rejection, or false guilt, is a stronghold. The Bible says in 2 Corinthians 10:3-4 that as disciple makers we are to help our disciples destroy these arguments and self-destructive thoughts. How do we do this?

The first thing we need to do is **Identify it**. You must name it. Every behavior is the fruit of a root. What is the root of our fruit? The root is thoughts. This is why we need to identify the thought that does not line up with the Word of God. This is why in Romans 12:1-2, we are told that transformation takes place "by the renewing of our minds." You need to name the root cause. Is it a fear, shame, blame, or rejecting thoughts? Is it failure? What does it sound like? Arguments usually sound like something like this in our minds: "I can't do it", "I am unworthy", "I am not spiritual enough", "What if I fail?", "What if they do not accept me?", "What if I start and don't finish?" You have to name it and help your disciples cast it out. The good news is that Holy Spirit will help us identify our weakness (Romans 8:26). The Holy Spirit is the flashlight in the dark places of our hearts. You are what you are because of what is in your mind. So if a lie masquerades as truth, we live in a lie. When you find something you want to do for God, but it gets in conflict with what you think you need, what you want is often going to lose out to what you need. And if what we think we need is based on a lie, then we will fail to live out the truth of the calling in our lives. Conquerors conquer arguments. It is a battle and war of words. Tearing down arguments is warfare. It is a battle because it goes to the very core of who you are. If you think you can't, you can't. But if you think you can because God says you can, then you can. The battle for your mind is a battle for your identity. If you want brave and courageous disciples, help them see themselves as God sees them. Destroy every lie that says that they can't.

They must also **Renounce it.** We must teach our disciples to reject and deject any of these false identities the enemy has convinced them to believe. Teach them to rebuke those thoughts in the Name of Jesus.

Declare it. Teach them to declare daily what God says about them. Before we conquer others, we must first conquer ourselves. Develop disciples who learn how to overcome discouragement by declaring what God says about their situation and trial.

The sixth trait is mentality. Disciple makers think differently because they are conquerors. They are able to see what others don't see. For example, when others saw a giant they could not defeat, David saw a giant he could not miss. Disciple makers understand that the bigger the blessing, the bigger the sacrifice. Their level of sacrifice will demonstrate what Jesus and his vision is worth to them. What your disciples think is contagious, whether godly or ungodly. This is why only leaders can raise leaders. Only disciple makers can raise disciple makers. Knowledgeable disciple makers understand that most potential disciple makers don't look or act like disciple makers when you first see them. Look at how God described David's recruits as those in "distress, debt and discontented" (I Sam. 22:2). But because they developed the seven key traits of a disciple maker, they were able to conquer kingdoms.

Qualities of a Disciple Maker

The type of future disciple maker you need to focus on are those who pursue your knowledge consistently and apply faithfully what they have learned from you. A potential cell leader is not a "loaves taker." Many people follow Jesus, the Master Mentor, because of the loaves he provided. Jesus gave to givers and sowed into sowers. Loaf takers can be manipulative because they seek to hoard things for themselves alone. Beware of those who do not pursue your teaching but pursue positions. They usually stop pursuing their mentor when their mentor stops pursuing them. You want to surround yourself with people who will be around you when you are imparting to others. They have to learn that others need your assistance as well; it cannot be all about them.

Seek out people who when their needs are met, continue to follow under your leadership. There are people who once their needs have been met, they no longer follow the vision and the mentor. Avoid people who only look for recognition.

Seek out people who have chosen to change by being around you. These are people who enjoy learning how to change from watching your life. Look for people who want to change to be prepared to be part of the principle of 12.

Seek out people who are willing to do what you have done to get what you have gotten. These potential cell leaders are those who are willing to make a commitment and pay the price to be a fully devoted disciple of Jesus. You will find different types of people coming to your cell group. You will either find those who come to take from you or learn from you.

Seek out people who look for wisdom that leads to progress. Some people, once they get a certain amount of wisdom, disconnect from their mentors. The prodigal son disconnected from his father when he thought he had enough wisdom to go on in life on his own, until he came to his senses and realized how good he had it at the palace of his father's wisdom. Notice how the father did not pull his prodigal son out the pigpen. Life's pigpen helps those under you to change their belief systems. The pigpen

114

is the place where character is formed and conviction is developed. Seek for those who have learned form the pigpen experiences in their life. Those are the ones ready to absorb all the wisdom that has been imparted unto you as a mentor.

Seek out those who have have consistently pursued mentorship from you. These are those who are as eager to start something, as they are to finish a project with you.

Seek out those who will not use familiarity to disrespect you. Free access does not mean that a mentor is to be disrespected by a protégé. The moment your protégé begins to follow a pattern of disrespect, you will find that that will be the day that he or she will stop receiving from you. Access is a privilege and opportunity granted to the person you are discipling, not a right or guarantee. They do not use the right to disagree as an opportunity to disrespect their mentor. Good protégés respect what their mentor respects when he or she is around the mentor. They recognize that they will keep serving as long as they keep respecting in the Lord.

A potential protégé is the one who will not use vital information to disrespect you. A protégé may be more up to date in a certain subject matter but he will not use it to disrespect you or to prove you wrong. They will use new and vital information to be an asset to your ministry and enhance theirs.

Seek out those who defend you, especially in the midst of false accusation or gossip. They act as a shield. This does not mean that you as a mentor should be protected from accusation if you are living a reckless and irresponsible life. The respect referred to here suggests that a disciple will not allow others to destroy your reputation based on a false report or rumor. These protégés feel so linked with you that they represent your reputation and honor. They protect respect!

Seek out those for whom your success matters. These are the ones that recognize that their success in ministry is tied up to your success in ministry. They rejoice when you succeed. They stay connected with you because they realize that their success has a lot to do with staying linked to your mentorship.

Seek out those who do not harbor offenses against you. Those who harbor resentfulness and do not communicate their true feelings are at best difficult to work with. You will become an offense to those who are not honest and truthful with you in ministry. Strife stifles mentorship like nothing else. Honesty breeds trust.

Seek out those whose loyalty is to their leader and not their peers. It has been said that the best protégé is the one who "is loyal to the chief and not to the Indians." Those who do not display loyalty become complainers and seek to tear apart leadership. A good protégé will report information that is often hidden by others. They are the ones who pull out the roots of division.

The Twelve Pillars of the Vision

God's vision of making disciples rests on twelve pillars. These pillars are values that you as a disciple should live by. Without these, you will eventually lose purpose and the joy of what you are doing in ministry. These twelve pillars are deeply held beliefs about the mission and mandate God has given you as a disciple of Jesus.

The twelve values of the vision are:

1. Call

The first pillar is the call. God has called every believer to go out and win this world for him. Look at the call of God in Isaiah 6:8 when the scriptures say, "Then I heard the voice of the Lord, saying, 'Whom shall I send, and who will go for Us?' Then I said, 'Here am I. Send me!'" God is still asking the same question to you and every believer today. In Matthew 28:18-19, we are told that the great call of God is to "go and make disciples." This is the
116

Great Commission. The reason why some people don't fulfill their ministry is because they have not answered the call. The reason why they have not answered the call is because they have not discovered their purpose.

Disciples of Jesus will never be completely satisfied until they fulfill their purpose. The problem today is many people in churches in America confuse their purpose with their function. What you do in church is your function, but the objective of all function is to fulfill your purpose. What is your purpose? Your purpose is to be fruitful and multiply. God told Adam and Eve "be fruitful and multiply" (Genesis 1:26). He told Abraham, the father of our faith, "be fruitful and multiply" (Genesis 1:26-28). We all have been called to the ministry (Ephesians 4:12) to do the work and to see the body of Christ grow through fruitfulness and multiplication.

I once was told a true story of the pastor's wife. She had a dream in which many people were coming to the Lord and bringing fruit to the Lord. And whenever they brought fruit the Lord would smile with approval. They were bringing baskets full of different kinds of fruits. These fruits represented people they had won and discipled to the Lord. When it was her turn to appear before the Lord, she came with a basket full of fruit. It was much bigger than everyone else who had come up to Jesus up to that point. She expected Jesus to be pleased with her offering but soon after she appeared before the Lord, tears began to come out of Jesus' eyes. As Jesus looked with disappointment to the pastor's wife and she became surprised that Jesus was not happy with her offering. With anger and self- indignation, she told Jesus "I can't believe you are not pleased with my basket full of fruit, what else did you expect?" Jesus then turned to her and said, "My precious daughter, yes, you brought a basket full of fruit, but this fruit does not belong to you, it belongs to your husband." The point Jesus was making was clear. We can't rely on the fruit of our pastors, father, mother, husband, wife, children or Christian friend. God expects you to produce fruit in your life (John 15:1-11).

The vision is a revelation of how God wants to use you to reach people. The calling of God is so important for you to realize because it is what God wants you to do while you are here on Earth. You will not have a supernatural drive in your life until you discover that you have been marked for ministry. Some people ask me, "How do you do it?" My question is, "How could you not?" You have been called of God. It is a personal call from God. God himself has put this special calling on your life.

Some churches today in America have fallen into the satanic lie that the only ones called to the ministry are pastors and evangelists. The scriptures tell us that pastors are called to train people in the church to do ministry (Ephesians 4). You will not find your passion until you get a revelation of your purpose. This is why the vision is a revelation from the Spirit of God. You will not do the vision until you realize that God has already called you to the ministry. Once you get a hold of this spiritual awareness, you will be passionate to do the vision God has already given you to do.

The commandments of God will become a delight instead of a duty when you enter into your purpose. Keep in mind that it is Satan's goal to derail you from your purpose. The call of God in your life is like a train, it only runs smoothly and speedily when you align yourself with the rail of God's purpose. This is why it is so important that you complete the School of Disciple Makers in your church. It will provide you the training you need to effectively and efficiently fulfill the call of God. In graduating from the School of Disciple Makers, you are saying to the Lord, "I love you Lord, I will fulfill my purpose to feed and shepherd your sheep" (John 20).

2. Courage

It takes courage to fulfill your purpose. Courage moves us from the comfortable to conquering. Where do you get courage? Courage comes from a vibrant and working faith. You will have all the courage you need when you live by faith. The faith that you need will only work when you trust in the promises of God. How do I get my faith to be fired up? Your faith will arise within you

118

when you make up your mind to trust in the promises God made to you in the Word.

In the vision your courage will be tested. Every man or woman of God who accomplishes something great has experienced times of tribulation and testing. If a disciple maker loses courage his ministry becomes paralyzed. Not only will he lack motivation and assurance but he also runs the risk of losing his disciples. Who wants to follow a leader who has no courage? In Joshua 1:9, we are told to "be strong and courageous."

The enemy knows that discouraged and faint-hearted disciple makers and leaders are a hindrance in the work of God. This is why Satan's plan is to place a seed of discouragement in your heart. How does he do that? He will tempt you to have you focus on the lack of expected fruit. We are vulnerable to discouragement when we start believing that results are not coming fast enough. Trust courageously that God will eventually give you a breakthrough, if you faint not. Courageous people stay the course.

3. **Connection**

The vision is about being connected. God has called us to be interdependent with each other. Who you are connected with will determine your success in your purpose in life. This is why you need a mentor and other disciples in your life. This is why every disciple needs a mentor in his or her life. It is also why we all need other disciples who will stimulate us into good works and a fruitful life. You need to be careful whom you get connected with in your life. The question you need to ask yourself is, "Who is speaking into my life?"

Where there is connection, there is honor. It is through your mentor that you learn to honor those over you. When you do not honor, you dishonor your ministry. God honors those who honor their leaders.

Why is God so interested in you being connected? God is interested in people. Ministry is about people. Church is about people. Disciple making is about people. If you are not making disciples, you are not interested in people. But you say, "I love the Lord." Jesus said, "If you love me, feed my sheep" and "If you love me, shepherd my sheep" (John 21:17). Listen to what Jesus is saying. You have not truly experienced what it is to fully love Him until you shepherd his sheep. Why? Because when you love people, you love the body of Christ. He said in Matthew 25:40, "Whatever you do to the least of my brethren, you have done it unto me." The way we love Jesus is by loving his people and staying connected with them.

There is no greater idea that God came with than the church. The church is the family of God. There is no business, government, nation, or anything else that Jesus blessed like the church (Matt. 16:18). God wants a family. In about 1,000 years from today Microsoft will not be around but the church will be here. Pepsi and Mountain Dew will not be around but the church will be around. Why? In Eph. 3:10 we are told, "So the manifold wisdom of God might now be made known through the church to the rulers and the authorities in the heavenly places." Are you hearing what God is saying? He is saying that only the church will last forever. It is through his people that Jesus will reveal what was God's intention after all.

When it comes to the church, we need to ask ourselves on a daily basis, "What's best for my church?" You should also ask yourself, "What's best for other churches?" Since we are going to live together forever in heaven as God's children, we must get along here on Earth. As a disciple, you must love God's family as he loves it. There are some people who use the church, but don't love the church. How do we demonstrate that we love the church? We show love in the way we spend our time, treasures and talents. It is the way you invest in these three that will demonstrate if your heart is really in the church.

As we connect with each other, we must learn to love one another. I am sure you learned during the holidays, when families get together, that no family is perfect. But though our families are not perfect, we love them and we stick up for them. Unfortunately, there are some Christians that spend all of their time criticizing other Christians. They have not learned that love is more important than their differences. If you love Jesus, you are on the same team as your fellow disciples. We are taught in 1 Timothy 1:4-8 that the purpose of instruction is not knowledge, but to love. The reason we learn is to learn to love one another.

Do parents enjoy when their children fight? Of course they don't; neither does God. We are forbidden at least five times in the Bible to argue with each other. We are also taught in 1 Corinthians 1:10 that we can't get everyone to agree in style, only in purpose. If we are going to effectively accomplish the work of God here in earth, we must all learn to go with the flow of what the Lord is doing in the local church. If you push on in the wrong direction of what the Lord is doing in your church, you are breaking the flow. When you flow, then you go with what God is doing in your church. We are warned in the scriptures that God judges people who bring division. Division breaks the power of synergy. Synergy is when we can do more together then when we would try to accomplish things individually. There is a momentum that occurs when we connect with one another that does not occur when we work separately, even if we are spending the same amount of time and effort. We are told in John 17:21 that the world will believe in Jesus when we stand connected as one. Avoid those who create conflict in the church like a plague. Make a stand. Loyalty is never silent. Speak up and expose any kind of behavior that causes division. Why? If you are not part of the solution, you end up becoming part of the problem.

The Lord takes division so seriously that he said to "reject a factious man after a first and second warning" (Titus 3:10).

Progression of connection

You may say, "But I am afraid to get close to people and get hurt." The reality is that everyone occupies a space in your life. The closer they are to you, the more vulnerable you are to them. The key is to manage your spaces with people in your life. Allowing someone to get close to you who doesn't belong there can lead to a hurtful experience. But having healthy relationships can be a tremendously enriching and rewarding experience. There is a progression of connection you need to understand, in order to protect yourself so that you don't get burned or do not make the mistake of positioning people where they don't belong in your life. Keep in mind that allowing people in your life is a process. Relationships follow a progression of connection. Let's take some time now to learn the progression of relationships.

According to Dr. A.R. Bernard, when we first meet someone, we enter into the INTRODUCTION stage. First impressions tend to be lasting, but they are not always correct. First impressions can fool you. You can begin with a positive first impression and end up with a negative experience or you can begin with a negative first impression and end up with a positive experience. So keep in mind that first impressions may be lasting, but not always correct. In the introduction stage we learn to know what people are like.

In the ACQUINTANCE stage, you go beyond the surface. This is where you learn a person's personality, intentions, agendas, where they are going in life, and whether you want to go there too. Only until you are fully complete this level, should a person allow someone to move to the next level.

The next stage is the FRIENDSHIP stage. This is the stage where you can make yourself vulnerable. The more you know each other, the greater the potential for someone getting hurt. It is a wonderful stage to reach as well. It is in the stage that we develop meaningful relationships. It is also in this stage that we find ourselves meeting the legitimate need for meaningful relationships. The question is not whether we should have friends or not but who we will choose as close friends. Who is a friend? A friend is someone who knows everything about you and chooses to stay connected with you anyway.

The last stage is INTIMACY. Few people who reach the friendship stage should ever make it to the intimacy stage. Every friendship does not and should not lead to intimacy. The ultimate form of intimacy is transparency. This is where we make ourselves emotionally and spiritually transparent to a select few. Physical transparency is reserved only for marriage. Emotional transparency should be limited to a few people in our lives. You will become intimate with whom you give yourself to. The problem occurs often when people want to go from introduction to intimacy and skip the other stages. There are people in your life that should stay at the introduction level. And yet, there are others who you should allow to move to the acquaintance stage.

Through the process of progression of connection you become yoked to a person and/or a group. We must choose wisely who to get connected with because you will have to carry the burden for whoever you are yoked with (Matthew 11:28-30). If you are connected to someone with a burden, their burden becomes yours. If someone is connected intimately with a drug addict, the problems that ensue because of his or her addiction will become their own. If someone is connected intimately with a dysfunctional individual, they will have to suffer the consequences of their dysfunctional lifestyle.

Don't be afraid to move to the next level when it is wise and right thing to do. You may ask, "What criteria should you use to allow people to move to the next stage?" The criterion is maturity. You will enjoy people when they are in the right place in the progression of connection based on their level of maturity. If a person is not mature and you allow them to occupy a space close to you, their immaturity will cause a crisis in the relationship.

If you find out that someone who is not mature enough is occupying a high place on the progression of connection, then you have a few options to consider. First, you can retrain them so they can come up to the maturity level required to handle the stage they are in. If retraining is not successful, you can reposition them. Place them in a space they are mature enough to handle. If the above two options do not work, maybe it is time to consider to retire them from you life. This is especially true with people who try to cause division and dissension in the body of Christ.

Jesus followed the progression of connection. He dealt often with the multitudes at the introduction stage. He had a group of 72 whom He was acquainted with. He had his G12, whom He called friends (John 15:14). Out of those twelve, He had Peter, James, and John, whom Jesus allowed to be in an intimate place in his heart. They were the only ones who were allowed to see him in His transfiguring splendor (Matthew 17:2). And out of His twelve, John the apostle was the closest to Jesus. When the disciples were curious as to who will betray Jesus, they asked John to ask Jesus (John 13:23-24). It is not coincidental that John was called the "disciple whom Jesus loved."

4. Cells

Cell groups are the small units of people in the church where discipleship and evangelism takes place. It is the easiest and most effective way to attend to the needs of church members. Cell groups are the best way to connect people with each other. It is the best environment for intimacy and bonding. In many churches you can attend for years and not know anybody in an intimate way. Why? It is nearly impossible to get close to people in a very large group without small groups where people can really get to know one another. This is why the first disciples started meeting in homes as the church started to grow (Acts 2:42-46, 5:42).

Cell groups help us close the back door of the church. How often we see people come to churches and fall through the cracks because of the lack of proper follow up! Even three hundred years ago, John Wesley, the founder of the Methodist church, understood the power of small groups when he said, "I was more convinced than ever, that the preaching like an Apostle, without joining together those that are awakened, and training them up in the ways

124

of God is only begetting children for the murderer. How much preaching has there been for these 20 years all over Pembrokeshire! But no regular societies [this is what they called cell groups], no discipline, no order or connection; and the consequence is, that nine in ten of the once-awakened are now faster asleep than ever."

Let's take a look how cell groups close the back door of the church.

Back Door A: Unreached Visitor

Some cell groups lose friends and family before they get to the cell group. Your cell group members, regardless how few or many, are a walking billboard publicizing your cell group. If they are loving and caring toward one another, unsaved friends will automatically assume that your cell group is full of acceptance and openness. If your cell group members are unkind or judgmental, their unsaved friends will assume that your cell group is full of hypocrites. As a cell leader, teach your group members that the best way to attract people to the group is through their living testimony. As the old saying goes, people don't care how much you know until they know how much you care. The best way to catch someone's attention is through an act of kindness or service. Teach your group members to do servant evangelism. Instruct them on the ways to target specific people in their neighborhood or job in a serving manner. For example, a person is much more willing to listen to your invitation to go to church, after having helped them out in carrying their groceries up to the fourth floor than if you just approach them cold turkey. Jesus declared that unbelievers will know we are the real thing when we show love towards one another. Remember, most people (around 86%) will come to your cell group or church because of an invitation from a friend or family member. When group members learn to open their hearts to outsiders, the non-churched people will start coming in.

Back Door B: The Guest

Cell groups are very effective ways of keeping guests connected with the church. We know that if a guest connects with a small group of people, they are very likely to stay in the church. People want someone who knows their name. Jesus told us in John 10:3 that a good shepherd "calls his own sheep by name." Jesus understood that people need someone who knows their voice. People don't want to be just a name in a church roster; they want to be known. Did you know that the voice of person is distinct from the voice of anyone else who has ever lived? It is as distinct as a fingerprint. People are unique and they need individual attention because they have individual needs, interests, and dreams. In small groups people get to know each other, thus creating strong relationships.

In your cell group, you will have different types of guests coming through the door. You may even have some that are already saved. The average church shopper visits around three or four different churches before making a decision about where they will attend. These types of guests are what we call "menu driven". They are interested in finding out what your cell group and church has to offer them. They are interested in find how their needs will be met through your cell and church. So take time to find out what their exact needs are. Are they looking for deep teachings or meaningful relationships? Are they looking to get involved in ministry or leadership? Are they looking for a strong youth group for their teenager or a children's church program?

You may also find others that have never been exposed to real Christianity. Most guests, especially unbelievers, come with a series of fears and anxieties. They are much attuned to their surrounding and how people in the group react towards them. Make it a point to approach a newcomer first. Don't wait for the guest to come to you. Show interest and genuine concern for them. Let them know that you are glad that they took time to attend the group. Most guests fear standing up while everyone else is sitting down. So when you introduce that new person to the group, do not ask them to stand up. It is very embarrassing for guests to do so. Guests also do not like to be forced to give. So if you have a guest, let them know that they are not obligated to give during offering time and that it is up to them to if they want to do so. Always let them know that they are welcome. Guests love to hear that word. By the way, if you have somebody assigned in your group to welcome guests, assigned the friendliest group member to do it. The last thing you want is Mr. or Mrs. Lemon Juice to be the first person a guest meets. Assign someone who you feel can best demonstrate the love of Christ to be the official greeter. This person is responsible for making sure that a guest does not feel isolated or alone. Guests do not come back a second time when they don't feel like they belong in your group. But the opposite is also true. When they feel like they belong, there is no one who will be able to pull them out of your group.

It is essential that you contact first time visitors within the first 24-36 hours. If you contact them within this time, there is a 50% greater chance that guest will come back next week to your cell group than if you wait longer than that. The more contacts the greater the possibility that they will come back. You may contact a person via phone, card, or home visit. People may come to your cell group for different reasons, but they will stay mainly because of one key element: a genuine relationship. And it is this relationship that must be initiated by the cell group leader and their group members. The more your guests feel connected to your cell group, the higher the likelihood that they will be back. If your guest comes the following week, he has a 50% chance that he will stay permanently in your group. If that person comes for a third time, there is a 75% chance that person is coming back. People who come after the third week want to know whether your group will continue caring and meeting their needs. If your group does, you have him for life! So the first three or four weeks are very important in terms of retention.

Following up with a guest is not a one-time event; it is a continual process of developing a mentor-disciple relationship. The deeper the relationship, the more likely the guest will stay in your group. If you help the guest make seven or more relationships between the cell group members and the church within the first sixth months, the person has a lower chance of dropping out of the cell group and church. But consider this, only 15% of those who have 3 or less friendships in their cell groups and/or church ever stay in a church or cell group. That is why cell groups are so vital.

Back Door C: Members

Do not assume that just because someone is a member of your group or church they automatically feel like they belong in your group. Church members who attend your group need to feel connected as well. They need to feel appreciated and not taken for granted.

If you see a change in group or church attendance, lack of involvement, or financial giving, you may have someone who is losing interest in your group. Sometimes you will hear a change in the way they talk about the cell group by saying, "your group" instead of "our group." They start losing group ownership. Some group members may become inactive when they face a trauma, hurt, or spiritual decay, etc. You are the first line of defense when someone goes inactive. If you feel that the situation requires further intervention, do not be afraid to consult with your leader.

Do not assume that you will find out the root cause for their inactivity on the first phone call. Expect to be doing more listening than talking. At first, you will hear numerous excuses, but what is important is to get the communication lines open again. Know that until the member feels that the situation is resolved or the need is met, they will probably stay inactive.

The longer you wait to reach out, the longer and more difficult it will be to bring them back in. If you don't reach out to them, they will assume that you don't really care about them.
Your cell group is the glue that will keep a cell member feeling like they are a part of the church.

5. Character development

In the vision of God, you are multiplying the character of Christ in others. It is the formation of the heart and mind of Christ. Our goal as disciples is to become like Jesus. Therefore, everything we do in the church and cell groups should ultimately lead our disciples to become more like Jesus. This has great ramifications. When you develop the character of Christ in others, you are restoring fathers to their children, reviving dry and dead marriage into blessed marriages, healing the hurt so they can become healers, changing the dissatisfied single person into a satisfied single person.

We are all multiplying ourselves one way or another. The question is, "What are you multiplying?" Are you multiplying faith, love, hope, joy, and perseverance, or doubt, bitterness, and discouragement? You will reproduce after you own kind. Cain reproduced (Genesis 4) generations of people whose names have a negative connotation, while his brother Seth reproduced generations of people who had names with positive connotations. Cain himself means "a lance or spear." His sons and grandchildren were Enoch ("translated to narrow disciple"), Irad ("fugitive"), Mehujael ("smitten of God") and Lamech ("wild man"). On the other hand, Seth's generations were men of character and fruitfulness. Seth himself means "appointed." His sons and grandsons, whom are mentioned in Genesis chapter five, were Enosh ("mortal man" – notice also that prayer began after his birth in Genesis 4:26), Kenan ("dwelling"), Mehalalel ("praise of God"), Jared ("descend" like humility), and Noah ("rest"). Imagine these were in your cell group; which of the two groups would you rather have? It is all dependent on who you are. Your cell groups will be eventually made up of people who will become what you are, not what you wish them to be. Why? Most things we learn in life are caught through our role models. So if you model the character of Christ, they will catch the character of Christ in you. You will reproduce after your own kind. You can only teach what you have learned and you will always reproduce who you are. You will download unto others your personal traits and character. You will transmit who really you are to them. This is why it is important that you allow your character to be formed and shaped by the Holy Spirit and by the mentor God has placed in your life as well.

If you want to shape the character of your disciples through the power of the Holy Spirit, you must believe in your people. Do not set limitations of what the Lord can do through your disciples. Most people who will come to your cell group will come with numerous sets of needs. Others will be what many consider "messed up". Your cell members will believe that they can change if you believe that they can change. Sometimes we don't believe in others because we don't believe on ourselves. We have our own insecurities and fears that we can't see beyond. Let the Lord deal with your fears, rejections, blame, shame, and guilt so you can clearly see what the Lord wants to do in your disciples through the power of the Holy Spirit. If you are not willing to receive instruction, correction, and deliverance from habits how can you expect your disciples to? Keep in mind that only God can change someone. We are simply vessels and instrument of divine change. If you keep this in mind, you will not frustrate yourself when change is slow in others.

Speak faith to your people and they will have faith. Speak dreams to them and they will dream the dreams of God. Speak ministry to them and they will do ministry as eagerly as you do. Speak disciple making to them, and they will make disciples. Your disciples will live to the level of your expectation. Regardless of where they are at in life, see them as God sees them. See your disciples at their full spiritual potential now. Those who expect the most, get the most.

Watch out for sin in your life. The number one reason cell groups don't grow or multiply is sin. Laziness, secret sins, gossiping, backbiting, bad attitudes, murmuring, complaining, sexual sins, and the like in your life are a recipe for a spiritual bacteria to affect the root of your fruit. The Lord says in Jeremiah 13:27, "How long will you remain unclean?" Deal with it quickly and decisively. The question we need to ask ourselves is, "What am I leaving behind from my character to those I mentor?"

130

Without character, your ministry will be crippled. Character does not make you a leader, but the lack of it can disqualify you. Andy Stantley said it so well, "Character doesn't make you a leader, but it does make you a leader worth following." There are only a handful of people in the Bible in whose lives were written about in detail and only good is said of their character and when they walked with God. One of them was Daniel. Through the life of Daniel we find that there is a process for character formation. The first step is to make a choice. The Bible says that Daniel resolved not to defile himself (Daniel 1:8). Character is a choice. Great leaders make the right choices and then support it as well. Daniel did not let the pressure of Nebuchadnezzar compromise his convictions or affect his decision. We learn from the life of Daniel that people who develop the right character do not wait to feel good before they do something; they do something before they feel good. Your choice will determine your actions, your actions will determine your habits and your habits will determine your destiny. An anonymous writer once wrote, "I am your constant companion. I am your greatest helper or heaviest burden. I will push you onward or drag you down to failure. I am completely at your command. Half of the things you do you might just as well turn over to me and I will be able to do them quickly and correctly. I am easily managed – you must merely be firm with me. Show me exactly how you want something done and after a few lessons I will do it automatically. I am the servant of all great men; and of all failures as well. Those who are great, I have made great. Those who are failures, I have made failures. I am not a machine, though I work with all the precision of a machine plus the intelligence of a man. You may run me for profit or run me for ruin – it makes no difference to me. Take me, train me, be firm with me, and I will place the world at your feet. Be easy with me and I will destroy you. Who am I? I am Habit!"

The next step in character formation is to confront conflict. A character conflict is when doing the right thing costs more than we desire to pay. Shadrach, Meshach, and Abednego, when asked to bow down in worship to an idol, said to the king, "If that is the case, our God whom we serve is able to deliver us from the burning fiery furnace, and He will deliver us from you hand, O king. But if not, let it be known to you, O king, that we do not serve your gods, nor will we worship the gold image which you have set up" (Daniel 3:18). In all conflicts where we are asked to compromise our convictions, there is one thing that God is looking for—obedience. Why? It is because obedience gives us access to the power and presence of God. What will keep our disciples from falling? The key is fear of God. We are told in Proverbs 16:6 that "by the fear of God men depart from evil." Work with your disciples in developing a healthy fear of God. No man can maintain a pure heart without the fear of God. If there is no fear of God, there is no fear of discipline.

The next level is change. Those who go through the process of character formation must be teachable and flexible. Only the teachable and flexible are bendable enough to change by the power of God. When change is necessary, to not change is destructive. There is a high price for low living. It is very important to keep in mind that refusal to change, when change is necessary, brings destruction to our lives. If someone is addicted to drugs and refuses to change, it will bring destruction. The same is true with any other vice or habit. If we refuse to change, growth and spiritual maturity will be lacking. If we are not growing, we are dying. Your growth determines who you are. Who you are determines whom you attract. Who you attract determines the success of your ministry. When a disciple does not want to be taught, he will not grow and connect with your ministry. What do we do when we confront someone who does not want to change? You can wet their appetite to change. We do this by showing our disciples the benefits to changing. The prodigal son came to his senses when he realized that his father's hired men had it better than he did (Luke 15:17). The last step is consistency. Daniel's character remained consecrated to God until the end. Integrity is consistency of character. Why is integrity important? What you are will outlast what men say you are. People buy into the leader before they buy into the vision. If they don't buy into your character, they will not buy into your commission, mission, and vision.

If you are going to maintain a committed walk with God, then you must have one holy passion. Stand faithful when others are fickle. Make a stand when others compromise. Just like in 1 Kings 18:21 when the Bible says, "Elijah came near to all the people and said, "How long will you hesitate between two opinions? If the Lord is God, follow Him; but if Baal, follow him." But the people did not answer him a word." The word "hesitate" in the text means literally "limp on the two divided opinions." These people were truly double-minded.

You will follow whatever or whoever is your god. This is why you have to make up your mind that the god you serve is the true and living God. Satan is happy when we almost do right. The people wanted to have both, God and Baal. We compromise when we conform. We conform when we think the same as the world. The world says, "I don't really need to go to church to be a Christian", "I can live how I want, it is my life", or, "What's in it for me?" We compromise when we make small concessions. You ever hear people say, "Well, I won't go to church today because is a bit cold, I won't pray because I am tired, or I won't go to cell group because one week won't affect me." You know you have the spirit of compromise when in the back of your mind there is still an option to do what you know you should not do. You must make up your mind that sin is not an option. The next time the devil or someone wants you to compromise, simply say to him or them: no deal. There will be no negotiation or bribe. The devil will try to bribe you with wealth or recognition. Never surrender to satanic suggestions. Those who decide to go all the way with God will be targeted with suggestions to compromise. And when the enemy can't get you through persecution, he will try pollution. He will try to pollute your mind with compromise.

Keep in mind that your private life will determine your public ministry. You need to examine your life and then examine your team. The high priest Eli lost his ministry because he did not confront his sons, who were committing open sin in the house of God. You may say, "What if I confront someone and they leave the church?" The reality is that they were going to leave anyway. As long as your confrontation was done in a loving manner, you did what was right and left the consequences to God. You and the group members are responsible to keep the sanctity of the group.

6. Conquering

What do we mean by conquering? Conquering is when you take the challenge of attempting something you never attempted before. In the Old Testament, they conquered territory, but in the New Testament, we conquer the hearts of men, women, youth, and children for God. The vision is about how God is reaching people now. It is about reaching your family and friends. It is about reaching your dreams for God. It is about conquering what the enemy had conquered and stolen from you and your family. The reason why we don't often conquer is because the enemy has conquered certain areas of our lives already. It is time to say, "Satan, the blood of Jesus is against you." It is time to say, "Satan, I am in the vision, out of my life." It is time to declare, "Satan, I am God's property, you are trespassing, I renounce you out of my life."

Soldiers are developed in boot camp but warriors are developed in the midst of the war. The same is true in God's army. There will be those who always flake out in boot camp and others who will retreat on the midst of the war. Don't focus your attention on those who flake out and are fickle. Focus on those who are with you. Conquerors don't focus on those who make excuses as to why they are not serving God; they focus on their God-given goals. Don't be intimidated by what you see, because we often miss what we don't see. We find this in the story of Elisha, when he was surrounded by a huge opposing army. The Bible says, "'Ah, my Lord, what will we do now?'" he cried out to Elisha. 'Don't be afraid!' Elisha told him. 'For there are more on our side than on theirs!' Then Elisha prayed, 'O LORD, open his eyes and let him see!' The LORD opened his servant's eyes, and when he looked up, he saw that the hillside around Elisha was filled with horses and chariots of fire" (2 Kings 6:15b-17). God is always working behind the scenes. Keep your eyes on the Lord. If someone happens to quit on you, know that God is in control and that He will give many more for everyone that leaves. People are sometimes around only for a season, others for a reason, and others are pillars. The only one that can stop you is yourself. Don't set limits on yourself. You serve a God of no limits. There is no territory or neighborhood that you cannot conquer in the name of Jesus. When champions take a blow, they simply try again. The enemy will attempt to cause you to give up by having you focus on discouraging results. Start each day by taking small steps toward your goal. Elmer Towns put it well when he said, "Future dreams are built on daily routine." Your daily routine of conquering your goals one step at a time will lead you to your future dreams becoming a reality. Don't avoid what you fear, but go after the very thing you fear that is stopping you from completing your assignment from God. Why? Whatever you avoid will dominate you. Whatever you fear will dominate you to the degree you avoid it. Know that that God has got your back. He will never fail you. God is on your side. If God is for you, who can be against you?

One of the most important things in conquering is your attitude. What is an attitude? An attitude is an inward feeling expressed by behavior. It is something happening in the inside that shows on the outside. Why is having the right attitude important?

Your attitude has presence. Attitude is what people remember about you (more than your singing, preaching, and teaching). Your reputation will begin with your attitude. It will determine your relationship with God, success in your ministry and job, promotion throughout life, how you will handle problems, family happiness, relationship with your leaders, and whether you will be joyful or not. It has the ability to draw or push people away. A healthy attitude helps you grow. The right attitude opens you to the Light: it can dispel darkness, discover dangers, and determine direction. What causes an attitude? Many Christians are held hostage by emotional and attitude strongholds. A stronghold is not an addiction. You can have a good stronghold or a bad stronghold. An addiction suggests that I am a powerless victim to my problem. The term addiction expresses the idea that something happened to me and there is nothing I can do about it. The term stronghold assumes a spiritual dimension. I can compare attitudes to a smoke detector. When a smoke detector goes off, it is not advisable to get a hammer and smash it because it is making noise. It tells you that there is something wrong and a fire has broken out. It is not concerned with itself. It is the same with attitude. Some people deny it or cover it up with distractions (pills, TV, recreation) so they don't have to face the alarm of their emotions. Some will cover it up with things such as food or entertainment. The smoke detector is to the house as your attitude and emotions is to your soul. Some people spend all the time with the smoke detector rather than locating the fire. Emotions are not what is wrong, they only tell you there is something wrong. How do you change your attitude? Let's look through 2 Kings 5:11-4 on how to change our attitudes. First, recognize that it is never too late to change your attitude (v.13-14). Next, evaluate your attitude (v.13-14). Then, you must desire to change (v. 13). You must also make an effort (v.14 "doe he went down and dipped himself"). Lastly, understand that you are just one thought away from your breakthrough (v. 11).

6. Vision lifestyle

You must embrace God's vision for your life as part of your lifestyle. What is the vision? The vision is the heartbeat of God, which is to bring people to the lordship of Jesus. God's vision is to see people saved from their sins. The vision of the Father was the passion of Jesus. You don't have the passion of Jesus, if your heart is not breaking for those who are damned to hell without Christ. Paul the apostle had this passion vibrating through his soul. In Romans 10:1, he says, "Brethren, my heart's desire and my prayer to God for them is for their salvation." Look also at his passion in Romans 9:1-3: "I am telling the truth in Christ, I am not lying, my conscience testifies with me in the Holy Spirit, that I have great sorrow and unceasing grief in my heart. For I could wish that I myself were accursed, separated from Christ for the sake of my brethren, my kinsmen according to the flesh." If you don't love the vision of the Father, your work for God will become a duty and not a delight. When you have a love for the vision, you will compel others to come and be saved. In Luke 14:23 we see an

136

example of this when it says, "And the master said to the slave 'Go out into the highways and along hedges, and compel them to come in so that my house may be filled.'" You must love the vision of the Father so much that you are willing to give your whole life to it (John 10:11, 13, 15, 17, 18). What drove Jesus to give His whole life to the vision of the Father was the lost sheep. Do you love the sheep enough to lay down your life for them? Do you love them enough to give all of your time, treasures, and talents to the vision of the Father? When you love the vision it becomes your lifestyle. Your greatest fear in life should be that you miss the purpose of God in your life.

The vision is not an event we come to, it is our life. Are you living the vision of the Father? Is your heart broken for the lost? If not, then ask God to give you His heart. The joy of heaven is to win souls. We are told in Luke 15:10 that "There is joy in the presence of the angels of God over one sinner who repents." If you are not passionately joyful about seeing souls saved, you have a pharisaic spirit, which is only interested in learning and not touching people's lives.

7. Work for the Lord

Most of the work in developing your cell group is at the beginning. We must not fall into the danger of just knowing much and not doing. If knowing alone was enough, why are 85% of churches in a declining mode, when we know more now in America than ever before? We have become professional religious talkers in America. But Jesus had deep and impacting words for those who talked the talk but did not walk the walk. Jesus put it this way: "Why do you call me Lord and do not do what I say?" (Luke 6:46). He also said, "But he answered and said to them, 'My mother and My brothers are these who hear the word of God and do it'" (Luke 8:21). In the book of James we are told to "Prove yourself to be a doer of the word" (James 1:22). The wisest man who ever lived, King Solomon, said in Proverbs 14:23, "In all work there is profit, but mere talk leads only to poverty." Profit or poverty will be determined by your level and intensity of work. If you don't work the harvest, you will not win souls for the Lord. The Bible says,

"The sluggard does not plow after the autumn, but begs during the harvest and has nothing" (Proverbs 20:4). From time to time you may hear someone say, "I am serving God my own way." The truth is that God will not bless a mess, stubbornness, stiff necks, or private agendas. The downfall of Israel is told in the very last verse of the book of Judges: "Everyone did what was right in their own sight" (21:25). Jesus said, "Follow me and I will make you fishers of men" (Mark 1:17). If you are not working as a fisher of men, you are probably not following Jesus the way He wants you to.

Shepherding is work. Jesus asked His disciples, "Do you love me? Feed and shepherd my sheep" (John 21:15). The vision of the Father requires work; it is not going to happen by chance. You can set goals, dream big dreams, pray, fast, and read your Bible, but unless you start working the assignment God gave you to win souls and make disciples, it is not going to happen. It is only going to happen if you start working the vision God has giving you.

God did not call you to be a pew Christian. The church in America is full of benchwarmers. God is calling you to get into the game. Some Christians are afraid to step up to the plate because they are afraid to strike out. But you will never hit home runs until you step up to the plate. Some people talk a good game, know the game, study the game, but they are not playing the game. It is time to get off of the pew and play the game.

8. Privilege
It is a privilege to be part of a team of twelve. Regardless of whether you are in the G12, G144, G1728 or any other group, it is an honor to be part of a team. Your position is not fixated by a title, but by the evidence of your fruit. Jesus gave us a powerful principle when He said, "You will know them by their fruit." The proof is in the fruit. God prunes branches that don't produce fruit.

Never allow an arrogant and prideful attitude to enter your heart regarding your position as a disciple maker in church. Though God has placed you in a position of authority, never make people

138

feel like you are superior to them. At the same time, don't walk around in false humility presenting yourself as someone without confidence and boldness. Understand that it is an opportunity and honor that God has granted you.. God has granted you favor; therefore, maintain an attitude of gratitude.

9. Cross

If there is one central message and focus point in the vision, is the centrality of the cross. The goal of every preaching, Encounter, and discipleship is to bring people to the cross. What do we find at the cross? We find redemption at the cross. It is the place where Christ took our place. He became the wrath absorber. He became a curse for us and made us the righteousness of God in Christ Jesus. The apostle Paul put the importance of the cross in the vision this way, "And when I came to you, brethren, I did not come with superiority of speech or of wisdom, proclaiming to you the testimony of God. For I determined to know nothing among you except Jesus Christ, and Him crucified" (I Corinthians 2:1-2).

The cross is the great equalizer. At the foot of the cross we are all sinners, regardless if you are wise or strong (v.18-31). No Christian should feel inferior, because when you have Christ, you have all of Him. However, at the cross we learn humility. The cross produces and promotes humility rather than arrogance and rivalry. At the cross there is no room for boasting and self-sufficiency. There we learn that it is not about you, it is all about Jesus. There we learn that in all we do we should give God the credit. At the cross we gain our assurance. Your faith is not based on an opinion of a clever person but on the sure proof of God's Spirit and power exemplified at the cross. The cross is not where people shine but where people die! God is not looking for show off, but God is looking for those to show off the glory of God.

You know that you have encountered the cross when you get to see your internal condition as God sees it in your heart.

The apostle Paul said, "I am crucified with Christ, and it is no longer I who live, but Christ lives in me…" (Galatians 2:20).

What does it mean to be a crucified man? The cross speaks of yielding. It is a place of surrender. A crucified man is one who has given control. When you give up total control to God, you yield to Him. And when you yield to him, you trust Him with everything.

The cross is the place of exchange. The cross is the place where we exchange the old for the new. It is the place where we decrease and he increases. It is the place where old things pass away and all things become new. It is the place where we trade our sorrows for dancing. It is where we no longer live, but Christ lives in us. What many people want in a church is accommodation and not transformation. There is no salvation experience until you carry your cross and experience death. Carrying your cross is not an option, but a requirement to salvation. It is not something we just do after salvation; it is what we do at salvation. Jesus put it this way, "And he who does not take his cross and follow after Me is not worthy of Me" (Matthew 10:38). You die to self-interest for you seek now God's interest. You die to self-ambition for you now seek after God's vision and dominion. You die to self-advancement, because you now seek the advancement of the kingdom of God. You die to self-dependence for you now take joy in being God- dependent. You die to self-absorption for you now are absorbed in His presence. You die to self-seeking because you now seek His face. You die to self-satisfaction and now you are fully satisfied in all that God is. The reason He first bids you to come and die to self is because self-centered people follow only themselves. You can only follow when you die to self-interest and you yearn to follow Him. You can only follow His will when you die to your will.

People who don't die to self-interest and attempt to do the vision are dangerous. They come with their own agendas and ambitions. Some want to make disciples to claim status and prominence. And yet others seek the attention of the crowd. Only those who truly give of themselves, to the cost of Christ, experience the fullness of the vision.

10. Multiplication

Be fruitful where you are. Multiplication can take place right where you are, even if the odds are against you. Some people are always looking and waiting for the perfect conditions, while they should be looking for what God is already blessing. Though Joseph was rejected by his family, friends, and foes, God gave him posterity and multiplication (Genesis 47:27). In the scriptures we find that every time God formed a twelve, there was multiplication that followed. Why? God always blessed those who follow what he is blessing.

Satan fears multiplication. He knows that multiplication makes a people mighty. In Exodus 1:7, we are told that the "sons of Israel were fruitful and increased greatly, and multiplied, and became exceedingly mighty, so that the land was filled with them." And then it says in verse 12 that the more Israel multiplied the more the enemy grew fearful. Like I mentioned before in this book, Satan fears synergy. Synergy is the interaction of two or more agents or forces, so that their combined effect is greater than the sum of their individual parts. This is why the Bible says that "one will put a thousand to flight, and two ten thousand." Multiplication is a threat to Satan.

Look at Satan's strategy to stop the children of God from multiplying. He first applied pressure. It says in verse 14 that Pharaoh "made their lives bitter." The enemy made work harder for them. He wants you to be so busy with the burdens of life and work that you don't have time to produce sons and daughters. He wants you working to the point of exhaustion in this world, so that you are too exhausted to father and mother children in the Lord. But this pressure did not stop God's children from multiplying. Pressures should never stop you from your purpose of multiplying. They made up their minds that nothing would stop them from multiplying. His second strategy was to make them sterile. Let me explain. He asked the midwives to kill the sons (v. 16). This is a form of sterilization. If they killed the sons, then there would be no males to mate with. He was attempting to intercept impregnation. The enemy today wants to stop those who will impart or "impregnate" the vision into those ready to receive. If there is spiritual sterility, then there will be no future generations. The enemy will stop at nothing to prevent God's children from reproducing spiritual offspring. Satan wants to sterilize you so you can't get pregnant with God's vision.

The Devil would rather fight with a few than with a multitude. He is an ex-employee of heaven and he understands the power of multiplication. Don't be surprise if the enemy attacks you when you are getting ready to start a cell group. He came against Jesus at the beginning of his ministry (Matthew 4). Those who seek to start a new generation of spiritual mentors and leaders will come under attack. The great news is that God will back you up. God backed up Israel and gave them a supernatural victory.

Multiplication is not a choice, but a divine command. From Adam, Abraham, Jacob, and others, God commanded them to multiply. Fruit is the commodity of the kingdom. It is what matters because nothing matters like people getting saved. The Bible is full of verses where God has called us to bear fruit and multiply (Genesis 1:28, 9:1, 35:11, Ex. 1:7, Mark 4:20, John 15:1-8, Colossians 1:6, Romans 1:13, Acts 6:7, 9:1, 11:21, 12:24, 14:21, 16:5, 17:12, 19:20). When you see a pattern in the Bible, you have a principle.

11. Fellowship with the Holy Spirit
You cannot do this vision without a supernatural move of the Holy Spirit. You can't win, consolidate, disciple, and send without the power of God. This is why you need to be a man or a woman of prayer and the Word. Balance your prayer life with the Word. Let me encourage you to keep a journal where you write all of the sermons preached at church and notes from the cell group teachings. Journaling is a great way to develop your spiritual growth and begin gathering principles and teachings that will prove essential and helpful when you start teaching your cell group. When you are in partnership with the Holy Spirit, your job is just to do what the Holy Spirit tells you to do. Let the Holy Spirit help you run your cell group meetings. Keep in mind that the Holy Spirit will never ask you to do something which is

contrary to the Word of God. Why? It is because the Word of God is the will of God. And the Holy Spirit will always support the will of God. The vision does not work effectively without effective praying and fasting. In all growing cell groups prayer and fasting is greatly emphasized. Join one of the many prayer meetings we run in our church. Prayer opens the door to God's power. If Jesus trusted the Holy Spirit, we should trust the Holy Spirit.

The New Testament church was a praying church. It is difficult to find a chapter in the book of Acts where someone or disciples were not praying. And look at the harvest they were able to reap! I found that one of the most difficult things to get Christians to do in America is to spend time in prayer. God's vision should stir you to seek Him like never before.

Effective cell leaders pray at least an hour a day (Matthew 26:40, Acts 3:1). Research conducted from the biggest churches in the world indicates that cell leaders who pray for their cell group members on a daily basis see greater growth than those who intercede for their group members only once a week. As Jesus prayed for His twelve, so should we.

If you have not received the baptism with the Holy Spirit, ask the Lord to give it to you. The disciples prayed and received the baptism with the Holy Spirit with the evidence of speaking in tongues (Acts 1:8, 2:1-4). It is this overflow of God in their lives that caused them to win the world for Christ.

Your relationship with your Senior Pastors

The Role of the Pastor
The role of the pastor is not only important but also crucial in the successful implementation of the vision of God in your life. This is true of any church attempting to fulfill the great commission.

Vision casting comes from the pastor. It is not something that the pastor can delegate to anyone else in the church to spearhead.

Vision casting from the pastor is important because the church will never outgrow beyond what the pastor is depositing into the hearts of the people. For this reason, among many other reasons, you need to stand with your pastors and support them in the vision.

In 1 Thessalonians 5:13, we are told how to support our pastors. In this passage you are given the principles in standing firm with your pastors to accomplish the work of God:

Principle of Appreciation: The word used here in this passage for "appreciation" literally means, "to know". You can't appreciate someone until you know them. Take time to find out what your pastors have gone through their years in ministry to get to this point. Know the pain and struggles they have experienced. You will appreciate your pastors when you get to know what it took for your pastors to be at this level of ministry. Most people do not have the foggiest idea of the struggle and burden that a pastor carries. A pastor is always mindful of God's flock, even on his or her vacation. People often make the mistake of criticizing a pastor because they don't have a clue what they go through. The average person can only keep up with their own family, but how is it that they are so quick to criticize someone who manages multiple families in the family of God? Stay thankful for the pastors God has given you. Appreciate what they do for you; then it will bring joy to your pastors and that is to your benefit. A joyful pastor is a pastor working out of strength.

Principle of Consistency: The apostle Paul says that there is one value he consistently asked for leaders to have and, that is to be diligent. Why? Because there is no other gift in the body of Christ that affects a local church like the pastor. If a pastor is not diligent, all will be affected by it at church. Since they must be consistent, your support must be consistent. Do not be consistent only when they are doing well, but through the difficult times as well. Be consistent through the good times and the tough times. Your pastors need you to finish as strong as you did when you started a project or an assignment from God. People who are consistent are not full of excuses, but of faithfulness. Your pastors don't need your excuses, they need your consistency.

Principle of Agreement: The Bible says, "How can two walk together unless they agree." You show support to your pastors when you enter into partnership with them. Paul says in 1 Thessalonians 5:12, "labor among you." This is a call to everyone to be in agreement in doctrine, purpose, and vision with their pastors. The Moses generation did not enter the Promised Land because they were not in a spirit of faith agreement with their shepherd Moses (Exodus 14:1-23). On the other hand, the Joshua generation conquered the Promised Land because they moved with a spirit of oneness and agreement with their shepherd Joshua. Which generation will you be a part of?

Principle of Honor: 1 Thessalonians 5:12 says that pastors "have charge over you in the Lord." Why? Your pastors serve as spiritual parents to help you grow in the Lord. Just like biological parents, spiritual parents have the authority to set standards, discipline, encourage, comfort, and belief in you. Some people struggle with the idea of being under the spiritual authority of someone else because they have unfinished business and issues with their biological parents. It is a transfer of unresolved anger and hurt. If that is you, let the Lord heal you heart from past hurts. Otherwise, you may bring those issues into your present relationship with your pastors. In Hebrews 13:17, we are told to "obey your leaders and submit to them, for they keep watch over your souls." There should be a sense of honor whenever your pastors share the Word of God with you. You also dishonor your pastors when you don't keep your word. Dishonorable people have a credibility problem and have an entitlement mentality. People who honor their pastors never curse what the Lord is blessing.

People will never protect what they do not respect. What you respect is ultimately what you seek to protect. I protect my parents because I respect them. I preserve the unity in the body when I protect my spiritual parents. God honors a church that protects the honor of their leaders. The brother or sister in the Lord who just stands by and does not take a stand for their leaders when they are criticized is just as guilty as the person making the remark. A church that stands for their leaders is a church that will be unstoppable.

Be careful of carrying an offense in your heart against your pastors. Never allow negative contamination or an argument in your heart against your pastors.

Principle of Esteem: In 1 Thessalonians 5:13 it says to "esteem them [pastors] very highly in love because of their work.". Some people love their pastors in a state of hypocrisy. They will tell their pastor how great a sermon he or she preached but as soon as they get into their vehicle they start criticizing and gossiping. What Paul is referring to here is your attitude. Your attitude can esteem or cream your pastors.

Principle of sacrifice: The bigger the blessing, the bigger the sacrifice. Your pastors need for you to sacrifice for the kingdom just like they themselves do. You can't expect your pastors to make all of the sacrifices while you just stand by as a spectator or a benchwarmer. The question sacrifice asks is, "Are you in it?" If you are, then it will show on your actions when your pastors call upon you.

Principle of Sharing: Always have the line of communication open with your pastors. If something ever ferments in your heart, simply share it with them. They will be more than willing to hear you out. Many times it is simply an issue of clarification regarding an issue. Try not to be oversensitive and take things so personally. Sometimes, a pastor will be sharing something from the scriptures and a disciple may feel that he or she is being targeted. Don't become egocentric. Understand that sharing is important in relationships. Without it, you will not develop a healthy relationship with your pastors.

Principle of Flexibility: Paul says in 1 Thessalonians 5:12 that your pastors "give you instructions." Be flexible enough to be molded through the words of instruction your pastors give every week. Don't ever allow your heart to become dull of hearing. Receive instruction with gladness in your heart. Someone once said, "Blessed are the flexible for they shall not be broken."

Principle of covenant: A covenant relationship is "a sacred agreement based on a pact to each other." God has always related to man based on a covenant. Communion also speaks of covenant. A covenant is most important to God and He despises covenant breakers. Jesus made a covenant with His twelve. The question for you today is, "Is this covenant with your pastors real?"

Chapter Five: How to have a Ministry of Multiplication

Take the challenge. In Matthew 25:14 we are told that the Master "called his own slaves and entrusted his possessions to them." He gave unto them with the purpose of having the servants multiply whatever was entrusted to them. God gives to you so you can multiply it. In fact, if God gives you something, He expects you to multiply it. The good news is that once you multiply whatever God has given you, He adds something else on top of your multiplication. In Matthew 25, we are told that to those servants who multiply, God gives more. God wants to move your ministry from glory to glory, faith to faith, addition to multiplication.

As a disciple maker, you add to your cell through evangelism and multiply through sending. You add members to your small group, but you multiply your efforts by developing those cell group members into disciple makers who will replicate what you have done.

Faithful servants are fruitful and multiply. He expects more than what you have now. But a key question you must ask yourself is, have you taken the challenge seriously? It is one thing to hear it, but it is another to be inspired by the challenge and run with it.

Increase your level of ability. (v. 15 "each according to his own ability") God is not asking you to do something you can't do. God has entrusted you with people and things to the level of your ability. But why does God only give you to the level of your ability? Because God will never give you something you are not prepared to handle. You can increase the level of your ability by reading books on leadership and discipleship, attending conferences, and listening to good quality preaching via DVD/CD or Internet. Keep in mind that your ability will determine your receptivity. Are you improving your leadership skills?

Check your heart. (v.23 "well done, good and faithful slave…" v. 26 "you wicked, lazy slave") If you have a heart problem, you will have a leadership problem. Just like a good lung cannot compensate for a bad heart, neither education nor talent will compensate for a bad spiritual heart. Never forget that whatever you allow in your heart will be expressed in your discipleship ministry. In the parable described in Matthew 25, the labor of the first two servants was a direct result of what was in their hearts.

Just like oil needs to be periodically checked in your car, your heart needs to be checked as well. Here are five things to check your heart for. Let's do a spiritual heart checkup right now by answering these questions:

Have you been feeling guilty?
Guilt says, "I owe you." Guilty people build walls and keep people out. This is not beneficial, since we are in the people business. If you stay in the land of guilt, you will end up being distant and distrustful of others. You will stay on the surface and not flourish in deep relationships. Guilt will mess with your conscience. A guilty conscience will take away your confidence and security like nothing else will.

Guilt says, "I am not worthy." Guilt can stop you in the middle of a prayer meeting and say to you, "You are not worthy to pray for this person." We are not referring here to a Holy Spirit conviction that produces a healthy form of guilt. The unhealthy form of guilt is when you have repented and confess your sins and you still feel guilty. The best way to deal with unhealthy guilt is to confess your sin and trust in God's grace. Stop relying in your own worthiness to be accepted by the Lord.

How is your anger level?
When someone is angry, he or she is saying, "You owe me." Their feelings are expressing what is in their hearts, which is, "I expect you to pay me back for what others did to me." The reason we often get angry is because we feel someone took something from us. Often, if we are not careful, we can enter into a payback mode when we are angry. We can become blame shifters. We find someone else to blame for our feelings and actions. We may end up punishing the failure of others. The problem with unresolved

anger is that it will end up developing it into a grudge. Private grudges result in public chaos. It is possible that you have an angry demeanor and don't know exactly what was taken from you, because the resentfulness and grudge has become part of you? There is only one true solution when dealing with an unresolved anger. The answer to unresolved anger is forgiveness. Forgiveness is canceling what people owe you. It is canceling the debt of an offense done to you. If you have unresolved anger in your heart, take a moment right now and let it go through the power of forgiveness.

How is your greed level?
Greed says, "I owe me." A sure sign of a disciple maker who is operating at the level of greed is the one who is reluctant to share credit and success with others. They make sacrifices for others, but only for the sake of personal achievement and interest. They struggle in moving others into the spotlight. The only solution to greed is generosity. Greed will destroy your ministry. Generosity will build your ministry. Who do you think people would prefer to follow, someone with a hidden agenda of greed or someone with the spirit of generosity who is looking out for the interests of others? Giving makes you face some of your deepest fears. Often when we try to make the transition from greed to generosity, a voice inside of us says, "If I give more, I worry that..." Generosity causes us to trust God for all our emotional, physical, and spiritual needs. This is why giving your tithes and offerings is so important, it breaks greed's grip on your heart.

How is your jealousy?
Jealousy says, "God owes me." Jealous people are often threatened by the success of others. They measure success by the failure of others. This is the type of servant of the Lord who often compares their ministry with others. There is nothing wrong from learning from other people's ministries, but it is unfruitful to compare your level of achievement with other ministries. Jealous people eventually take it out on God. When they begin to compare their level of success with others, and interpret their apparent lack of success as God owing them something, they begin to say "It is

not fair, why does this person have more, is more blessed," etc. Jealous people often allow other people's talents to play into their insecurity. The only way to deal with jealousy head on is to celebrate others. Learn to celebrate publicly whatever threatens you privately.

How is your fear level?

Fear speaks. It always says, "I can't." In the Parable of the Talents (Matthew 25:25), the servant said, "...I was afraid." Fear often causes procrastination among those who are controlled by fear. Notice how the one who multiplied moved "immediately" (v.16) into action. Fear paralyzed the other man's multiplication opportunity. The quickest way to get rid of fear is to activate your faith. Faith will paralyze fear dead in its tracks. Faith does not fear taking risks like the other two faithful servants did. Are you paralyzed by fear? Just believe!

Stop operating at the level of inferiority

If you are going to have a ministry of multiplication, you must overcome inferiority. Inferiority says, "I can't", "I will fail", "be realistic", and "nobody believes in me." It is the voice of accusation. Inferiority is dangerous to your spiritual walk because it kills the spirit of conquest. The Devil loves for you to pray, "God I am not good enough to serve you." He loves to hear you say that you don't have what it takes to do the vision. The enemy loves for you to stay at this level because, if you are operating at the inferiority level, you can't lift up anybody else.

Keep in mind that people will see you as you see yourself. Listen to how the children of Israel described themselves, "we *became* like grasshoppers in our own sight, and so we were in their sight." My question is, "How would they know they were like grasshoppers in their sight, if they never spoke with the giants?"

Never accept the idea that you are less than others. You are not the opinion of others. The answer to inferiority is a sound mind. A sound mind is a mind that has a right view of self. He or she understands who they are in Jesus Christ. Every day you should confess what they Bible says about you. You should declare, "I am fearless", "I am secure in Jesus" and "I have everything I need in God." Do you have the DNA of inferiority or the DNA of a sound mind in God's vision?

Turn your focus on those who are sons and not the slaves
Disciple makers who multiply have sons and not slaves. Slaves are those who do the work of God out of duty, but take no delight in their shepherds. It is a job for them, not a jam! Sons in the ministry are those who do the work of God out of a joy in the Lord.

What makes one become a son and another a slave? The answer is fear. Fear is tied to the spirit of slavery. Relationship and mutual respect is tied to sonship. True sons say, "Here I am to stay." Sons feel like inheritors. True sons and daughters seek to find the secret of the anointing in their spiritual parents but slaves seek to compete instead.

How do you know if you are a father or master? The answer is if you take you joy in meeting with your people. It is like when Paul said in 2 Thessalonians 2:4, "longing to see you...so that I may be filled with joy." If you find somebody is constantly clashing with you, you don't have a son. You know you have a son when you both have one heartbeat. The test of your relationship will occur when you disagree with your disciple or cell member. Every relationship is tested. When it is tested, sons stay with you. Sons will search you out (II Thess. 2:17) and will refresh you (v.16). A wise disciple maker will spend more time with sons in the ministry than with those who just do the work of God out of duty.

There must be a dying process before multiplication can occur
In John 12:24, Jesus said, "Truly, truly, I say to you, unless a grain of wheat falls into the earth and dies, it remains alone; but if it dies, it bears much fruit." Jesus, in essence, is saying, "If you are going to be fruitful in following Me, it is going to cost your life; it is going to cost you absolutely everything." The truth is that the only thing worth living for is the one passion that is worth giving my whole life to, and that is Jesus. And there must be a dying to your

fear, doubts, selfishness, laziness, passivity, and sin in order to do so.

Where your roots draws life will determine the size of your ministry

In Psalms 1:1-3, we learn that as disciple makers we need to be connected to the rivers that flow out of the Holy Spirit. Let your roots go down to the current of the Holy Spirit. We do this by going deep in the Word, prayer, and fasting. Avoid contaminated waters. Keep away from people who will contaminate you with negativity, self-doubt, and insecurity. Watch out for scoffers and mockers. They have within them an infectious doubt. Mockers are doubters. Though appearing intellectual, they have a defective faith. Mockers will dry you up if you sit and commune with them. Draw from what God wants to do in your life through the power of the Holy Spirit and in due season you will be like a tree bearing fruit. Don't underestimate the potential within you in Christ through the power of the Holy Spirit. Just like the seed has a tree potential, you have a multiplication potential through Christ's anointing upon your life. One thing is for sure, if you draw from God's river, God's program cannot fail in your life.

Develop an abundance mentality

A disciple maker who has an abundance mentality believes that others can dream the impossible. They believe others can become the best leaders they can be. Those who don't have an abundance mentality will continue to have doors close on them as long as they are attempting to get people to give them all of the credit and attention. Those with an abundance mentality live in the overflow. They never think, "I don't have enough."

Those who multiply become a source of wisdom and knowledge. They learn as much as they can, as aggressively as they can and as best as they can to become they want to be make others bigger, broader, and better in their ministries. Disciple makers who multiply are more than just a headline. They are not shallow in their knowledge of the Word of God. Disciple makers who multiply are committed to reading good books.

153

Disciple makers who love people read books. Why? Those who read commit themselves to give the knowledge that they receive away. Disciple makers promote the growth of their disciples by sharing what they learn.

Those with an abundance mentality also understand that there is no multiplication without connections. Your network is based on connections. Your network is your net worth. You will accomplish more in the next three months developing a sincere interest in three people than you will accomplish in three years by trying to get three people interested in you. A network is two or more people tied by a relationship and focused on a common vision. As you build your network of disciple makers as you build your group of twelve, keep in mind that those who appear powerless or insignificant may be stars waiting to rise. Believe in the least and the last. Believe in those nobody else will give an opportunity to be involved in ministry. They will remember that you were on their side when nobody else was.

Become like Jesus

The biggest secret of multiplication is to become like Jesus. John 15 tells us that the more you abide in him, the more you become like him, and the more you become like him the more you will bear fruit like him. If you abide in Jesus you will "bear fruit" (v.2), "more fruit" (v. 5) and "much fruit" (v.5). The reason why some people do not bear fruit like Jesus is because they have not become like Jesus. The more you become like Jesus the more compassion you will have for souls. The more you become like Jesus, the greater the progression of bearing fruit you will have. The person who is becoming more like Jesus needs very little motivation because he is just living who he or she is in Christ. When you become more like Jesus, you will witness and win souls more like Jesus. When you become more like Jesus, you will make disciples like Jesus. When you become more like Jesus, you will pray like Jesus. When you become more like Jesus, you will talk more like Jesus. And, when you become more like Jesus, you will treat people more like Jesus. This is why the disciples were soul winners and disciple makers, because Jesus was a soul winner and

154

disciple maker (John 4:1). God the Father had only one Son, and he was a soul winner and a disciple maker. Shouldn't you be as well?

Breaking the spirit of discouragement and failure
The enemy's plan is to contaminate your spirit with doubt, discouragement, and a spirit of failure to make you think that you are a has-been, a reject, and a no good disciple of Jesus. The Devil wants to infect your heart with words of discouragement and failure, so when God gets ready to withdraw from what has been deposited in you, it will be poisoned by a spirit of failure and discouragement.

The disciples of Jesus experienced discouragement and failure in their lives. At one time they came back from fishing all night long and came back with nothing. In the morning they were washing their nets because they had given up on catching fish. It is like some in the ministry who have worked long hours in trying to fish for men and women and come back empty handed. They begin to allow a root of discouragement and failure to take hold of their hearts. The spirit of failure says, "Nothing else is going to happen." Have you been washing your nets lately? There will be times, just like with these disciples that you will be tempted to just stop fishing and start washing your nets. Washing your nets is an indication that your expectations have been destroyed. If you find yourself washing the nets, you have come to believe that what your ministry is currently is all that it's ever going to be.

Those with a spirit of failure feel that their faith has been muffled. They find it difficult to clap their hands after a message, sing songs during worship, and take notes in church. They have come to believe that things are not going to get any better. If they are not careful, they may find themselves saying, "I am through trying."

The good news is that in Jesus no failure is ever final. Your failure is never fatal and your failure may be the start of your future. Why? It is because the God that you serve has a kingdom agenda for you. You have a mighty calling from God. Through Jesus, you are greater than your circumstances; you are much better than your condition. God's destiny cannot escape those who are in Christ Jesus. You have been marked with God's purpose. In God, failure is not an option. This is why you feel God pulling you out when failure tries to pull you down. Since you are on an appointed assignment from God, you cannot fail. Yes, you may go through seasons of pressure, a lack of apparent success, but failure is not an option when you are in Jesus. Who told you God was not going to make your ministry fruitful? Who told you that you would not catch multitude of souls for the Lord? It was certainly not God. It is the enemy of your soul, Satan, who keeps telling you that you will fail if you try. But the Devil is a liar. It is not over until God says it is over. In spite of adversity, in spite of opposition, it is not over. Just like with the disciples were at the lake, God is going to give back what you have given.

Failure is something you do, not something you become. There is a vast difference between the man who said, "I failed three times," and the man who says, "I am a failure." One ball player set the major league record for strikeouts with 1316. The same player set a record for 5 consecutive strikeouts in a World Series game. But he became one of the greatest baseball players to play major league baseball: Babe Ruth. Some Christians today are so worried about striking out in ministry that they don't even swing to make a hit for God.

In this passage we find out what we need to do when we feel like a failure and discouraged. The first thing we need to do is to launch out. Jesus calls us out to go into the deep. Get away from what is shallow in your life. Get away from shallow people, shallow purpose, shallow vision, shallow thinking, shallow commitment, shallow prayers, and shallow dreams. People who stay on the shore find themselves fearing failing again. But it is when we go into the deep that we can catch the multitudes of souls.

When we succumb to the spirit of failure, we can fall into the danger of getting insulted when others attempt to speak into our life. If you ever feel like you are a failure, talk to your cell leader

156

and let them speak words of encouragement that will launch you out into the deep again.

Peter had the right response when Jesus told him to go into the deep. Peter said, "Master." Peter knew that if anybody can do it, it was Jesus. When you feel discouraged, let Jesus be master of whatever apparent failure you are facing. Jesus is in total control because He is the infinitely great God. Jesus is the Master over sickness, materialism, multitudes, marriage, ministry, and Master over everything.

Second, you need to have a nevertheless attitude. A nevertheless attitude means that regardless of your opposition and failure, you will continue to believe God for your miracle catch of souls. Apparent failure is only temporary; giving up is what makes it permanent. Next time you face discouragement, speak to your circumstances the Word of God and say, "Nevertheless."

Next time you hear the words of discouragement and failure, hear the word of God that says to you, "Try it again." Think about it: if God told you to do it, it must be important. God did not bring you this far to leave you and He did not bring you this far to let you down. When you don't see immediate results, and you feel like giving up on ministry, God says, "One more time."

The third thing the disciples did was drop their nets. Take notice that this passage says that they dropped their nets, not they dropped their net. He uses the plural form. It indicates that they had a large catch. Jesus was teaching us here a valuable lesson. The situation is bigger than you think. We tend to limit God. Peter uses the singular, but Jesus uses the plural form of the word net. It may not make sense right now why the Devil has fought you so much with doubt, discouragement, distractions, and disappointment, but it is bigger than what you think. Drop your nets. Move into action again because it is bigger than what you think. Win souls again because it is bigger than what you think. Consolidate disciples because it is bigger than what you think. Disciple your disciples because it is bigger than what you think. Send out disciples because it is bigger than what you think. Don't stop praying because it is bigger than what you think. Don't stop fasting and reading your Bible because it is bigger than what you think. Don't stop doing the vision because it is bigger than what you think.

Remember, Satan is after your faith. Satan is in the business of discouraging believers. What is Satan's strategy? He has a threefold strategy to get you discouraged.

He first wants to dismantle your faith. Satan will attempt to dismantle your faith through fear. What is fear? The anatomy of fear is very interesting. Fear comes from speculation. Speculation comes from uncertainty. Uncertainty comes from a lack of control. Fear is a failure to see that God is in total control of the situation.

Fear is a failure to comprehend that God is in complete control of everything. You fear when you fail to relinquish control to God. As stated previously, the opposite of fear is faith. They both have their own sets of languages, expressions and manifestations. The problem with fear is that it breeds self- doubt. In the book of Nehemiah, we find a good example of this. During the time when Nehemiah was trying to rebuild the walls of Jerusalem, the enemies of Nehemiah were attempting to undermine his confidence by saying, "Can they bring stones back to life?" (Nehemiah 3:1-3) In other words, they were saying, "Not a chance!"

You begin to doubt yourself when you stop praying. Why? Because when you stop praying, you stop listening to the voice of the Lord and start listening to the voice of the critics. So what do we do?

Nehemiah Principle #1: When Satan attempts to dismantle your faith, pray. Did you know that Nehemiah prayed four months prior to approaching the King with his petition? He prayed throughout his entire satanic struggle (Nehemiah 4:4, 9, 10; 5:19, 6:9, 14). In every chapter of the book of Nehemiah, we find a struggle and test, but we find him praying and not panicking!

158

Prayer is the answer to fear. If lack of control is the genesis of fear, then God's greatness is the genesis of faith. Look at verse 14, how he reminds them of God's greatness. In prayer we see God's greatness as more important than our weakness.

Second, Satan will seek to demoralize your spirit. What normally demoralizes people's spirit? The first way he seeks to demoralize your spirit is through ridicule (v. 4). Thomas Carlyle once said, "Ridicule is the language of the Devil." He loves to belittle your attempts for greatness. He also seeks to put pressure on you (v. 7-8). It is so difficult to feel uplifted when you face pressures in life. He is also a specialist in making threats. Satan's sneak attack is intimidation. The devil loves to intimidate people by applying pressure. The Bible says that they were approached ten times. The number ten is the number for a testing period. The enemy will be consistent in attempting to wear you down with pressure. Satan's strategy also includes burnout (v. 10-12). Burnout occurs when we don't see success fast enough. Fatigue, frustration, and fear are the cocktail of burnout.

Nehemiah Principle #2: When Satan attempts to demoralize your spirit, persevere. In Nehemiah 3, it tells us that they continued working past their normal working hours. They persevered regardless of the opposition. Calvin Coolidge said it well when he said, "Press on." Nothing can take the place of persistence. Talent will not. Nothing is more common than unsuccessful men with talent. Genius will not. Unrewarded genius is almost a proverb. Education will not. The world is full of educated derelicts. Persistence and determination alone are the overwhelming power.

Satan's last bombshell is to distract your focus. Whatever has your attention has your focus, and whatever has your focus has your heart! What is diverting your attention? Is it your past, unhealthy relationships, secret sin, greed, problems, or financial circumstances?

Nehemiah Principle #3: When Satan attempts to distract your focus, stay purposeful. What was the ultimate purpose of

Nehemiah experiencing all of these tests of discouragement in this story? When everything had been said and done, God did it (Nehemiah 6:16).

Your ministry will rise to the level of your faith. Set your level of faith based upon God's promises and not on people's doubt. If you accept people's justification for their low level of faith, you will end up living with a low level of faith. Let your level of faith rise and your team's level of faith will rise. Don't ever allow somebody's shrinking faith to inhibit your largeness of faith. Your ministry and team will rise to the level of your ability to obey God's voice quickly.

To conquer discouragement and the spirit of failure, you must take hold of your thought life. Everything in your life begins with a thought. What you think determines who you are and who you are determines what you do. Your thought life determines your ministerial destiny and your ministry determines your legacy. You are today where your thoughts have brought you. So if you find yourself in depression, the thoughts you are entertaining have brought you there. If you don't like where you are today emotionally or spiritually, then you must change the thoughts that brought you to this place in life. Who you will become tomorrow in ministry will be determined by where your thoughts take you. Nothing limits fruit like small thinking. Nothing breaks the limits off of your life like no-limits thinking. You never achieve higher in your ministry than your thought life dictates. So watch your thought life. Don't allow negativity, doubts, complaints, arguments, or unbelief nest in your thought life. Learn to renew your mind with God's Word daily (Romans 12:1-2).

Goals that make a difference
As a disciple maker, setting goals is a very important aspect in establishing a ministry that will grow and multiply. What is a goal? Pastor Bray Sibley says, "A goal is a target of your faith." In the Gospels, we find that Jesus set goals. To accomplish His goals he made plans. What is a plan? It is a written list of
160

arranged actions necessary to achieve your desired goal. The Bible says that we are to "...write the vision, and make it plain upon tables that he may run that readeth it" (Habakkuk 2:2). Jesus planned for your future years ahead of time (John 14:2). God the Father scheduled the birth, the crucifixion, and resurrection of His Son before the foundation of the Earth (Rev. 13:8). He even scheduled a meal, the marriage, and the supper, six thousand years ahead of time! Think about the fact that the Bible is the plan of God for you. God always honored men who planned because those who fail to plan are simply planning to fail. Nehemiah planned exactly how he was going to rebuild the wall of Jerusalem, even in the midst of opposition and God granted him favor (Nehemiah 2-4). Noah had a detailed plan of building the ark and God granted him favor. Each day spend time writing down what you want to accomplish. If you don't write it, most likely you will not do it. When you write it, it is ever present before you. Don't rely on memory, since the pressing needs of life can get us focused on something else to do. We can end up majoring in minors and minoring in majors if we don't write down what we need to do in the order of priority. Make sure you assign each task to a specific time.

Successes in ministry and personal life are usually scheduled daily events. For those who don't take time to plan, consider this: sometimes you have to do something you dislike or would want to postpone, in order to create something you love. Since the secret of your future is hidden in your daily routine, make sure that your daily routine is planned out. Learn from the ants, for even they think ahead (Proverbs 6:6-8).

Jesus always had a passion for his goals. The scripture says this about Jesus' passion: "For the Son of man is come to seek and to save that which was lost" (Luke 19:10). We are encouraged to "whatsoever ye do, do it heartily, as to the Lord, and not unto men" (Colossians 3:23). Find something in the vision that consumes you and do it. Your duty is to delight in the goals God has given you. It is a choice to rejoice. It is a choice to have joy. Choose to have an attitude that says, "This day belongs to God and His vision and I can't wait to accomplish the goals God has given me to complete."

Jesus established specific goals. Jesus knew that champions are detail oriented. He explained it this way, "For which of you, intending to build a tower, sitteth not down first, and counteth the cost, whether he has sufficient to finish it?" (Luke 14:28). Set SMART goals which are Specific, Measurable, Achievable, Realistic and with a Time frame. Once you create them, post it somewhere so you can see it on a daily basis, pray and envision it coming to pass by the Lord. You may even want to create a collage where you place pictures of what you want to accomplish.

Jesus set out to finish what He started in the ministry. Conquerors and champions are finishers. They are not satisfied with just having a great start, but a strong finish. Pursue your goals to completion. Jesus did. At the cross, He redeemed mankind and was able to declare, "It is finished" (John 19:30). Great men and women of God complete what they start (2 Timothy 4:7, 1 Kings 6:14).

Jesus carefully watched over His personal schedule. Jesus did not allow anybody to set Him off course. Often, Jesus would say, "It is not my time." He knew exactly what He needed to do and when to do it. Watch out for interruptions. Your daily planner is your life. Time is one of your biggest commodities. You cannot save or collect time; you can only spend it either foolishly or wisely. The Scriptures tell us, "A wise man's heart discerneth both time and judgment" (Eccl. 8:5). You can guard over your personal schedule by setting your list of priorities. Jesus did not allow others to get Him off track. If you do, it will derail you from accomplishing what you must. If you don't fill your schedule, somebody else will. Protect your schedule because this is your life. Jesus knew that God would get greater glory if He stayed on God's schedule.

Jesus determined the end. He determined what He wanted to see come to pass. This should be included in your goals. At the end of the day, what is it that you want to accomplish? At the end of the month, what is that you want to see come to pass?

Let me give you some examples of goals you can set for yourself in the work of God. You can set a goal to bring three new people to church in a month. Then, set a goal to bring all three to the next Encounter weekend. Next, establish a goal to enroll those people in the Post Encounter.

Make up your mind about your goals. Once you establish your goals, make up your mind to do it, no matter how difficult it may seem in the natural. Take your "but" out of the way. When you take you "but" out of the way, you will experience no hesitation. Expectation with hesitation leads to frustration. When you remove all the "but", there will be no procrastination and no man-made limitations. Do not become a double-minded man or woman (James 1:8). There will be battles of your mind. You will experience a war of words. What you need to do is speak to your doubts and listen to your faith. Set supernatural goals that will bring glory to God. Supernatural goals are those in which only God is able to bring them to pass. This is why only He would get the glory.

Dream big dreams
Goals come from dreaming God's dreams. God has given every believer a dream of posterity. In Genesis 1:28, God promised and commanded Adam: "He blessed them" and said, "be fruitful and multiply." The only things that did not reproduce in creation were those things that were dead! This is the first command God gives to man. It indicates how vital and important it is. The blessing is in the command. The dream was in seed form in the promise. God's intention for everything that has life is to reproduce. If you have life, you should be spiritually reproducing. The inner dissatisfaction you felt this year was the inner yearning to fulfill your purpose. Your purpose is to reproduce and have posterity. God did plant a dream in Abraham's heart. In Genesis 17:2, God told Abraham, "I will establish My covenant between Me and you, and I will multiply you exceedingly. For I will make you the

father of a multitude of nations" (v.5). What God promised Abraham, he promises to you to also (Galatians 3:14, 29). You will hear at times people who will say, "I have not time for this." Unavailable people have small dreams because they are too busy pursuing their little plans. Unavailable people become spiritually sterile. God has given you a specific task and a sacred trust. God has called you to be a gardener and a guardian of souls. There is nothing worse than a person who has a dream with awesome goals from God who becomes idle.

God has given you a garden. Are you working your garden? Everyone has a garden to cultivate. Is your garden full of weeds or fruit? Weeds are often a sign of neglect. Dare to start dreaming of a garden that will bear much fruit for the glory of God. Start dreaming about people who will become fully devoted disciples of Jesus Christ. Start dreaming of your group of twelve this year. Then, dream of your G144 and so on. The day you stop dreaming you start drifting.

The vision is a spiritual concept and therefore it must be conceived in your spirit by the Spirit of God. Joshua was only able to enter into the land of fruitfulness after the twelve were in one agreement with the vision. It must be downloaded from the Lord to you and your future twelve as you get ready to enter the land of multiplication. When Jesus revealed himself to the disciples after the resurrection, Thomas, who was one of Jesus' twelve, was missing. Notice that Jesus came back for Thomas so that he could be on the same page with the rest of the twelve. Jesus wanted the twelve to move with the same dreams, goals, and vision. He wanted them to have the same revelation. If you have an argument in your mind against the vision of 12, this will lock your mind from receiving everything that God wants to impart through this method. If you don't mentor your twelve into the vision, you are not going to succeed. You must renew the minds of your twelve in order for them to be victorious. They must learn to dream the dreams of God. Pastor Cho said, "Dreams are the language of the Holy Spirit."

There are people who will come to destroy or deflate your God-given dreams. But these arguments can be easily destroyed by showing them the Word of God. Here are four principles from the Word that solidify the fact that God's vision is to be done:

Four Things That Can Destroy Every Argument Against the vision

Our <u>mission</u> as Disciples of Jesus Christ is the same as His: To change the world.

Our <u>method </u>as Disciples of Jesus Christ is the same as his: To win, consolidate, disciple, and send.

Our <u>model</u> as Disciples of Jesus Christ is the same as his: To raise up twelve.

Our <u>motivation</u> as Disciples of Jesus Christ is the same as his: The burning compassion of God.

Since your dreams are based on a biblical foundation, you should never allow anybody to blur your God-given vision. And, since dreams are Holy Spirit-given goals, let it saturate your soul with joy at the very thought of them. You must guard against tampering by others. You will become your dream and whatever you dream will determine your destiny. Your dream is your unfolding future. This is why the enemy tries so hard to tap into your imagination, fantasies, and dreams. A dream drives you and draws you to God's destiny for your life. We find in Genesis 12 that Abraham was drawn by a dream and vision that God would "make him a great nation" (v.2) and that in him "all the families of the Earth will be blessed" (v.3). What I love about God-given dreams is that they are always bigger than you (all the families of the Earth will be blessed), you can't let it go (Abraham stuck to this promise for 30 years), you must be willing to give everything to it (Genesis 12:4 "So Abram went forth as the Lord had spoke to him"), it will last forever, it will meet a need nobody else has met, and it will bring glory to God (Romans 4:20).

Don't let your past dictate your future. Let your past be your past. Otherwise, you will always be tempted to go back to where you came from. A person without a dream will always be tempted to return to his past. When Judas lost his dream of reaching this world for Christ, he returned to his greedy ways. We find a man in the Bible whose name was Demas and he served the Lord. In Col. 4:14, Paul makes mention of him when he said, "Luke, the beloved physician, sends you his greetings, and also Demas." But by the time we find him in II Tim. 4:10, Paul tells us that he returned to his past, "…for Demas, having loved this present world, has deserted me and gone to Thessalonica…"

Many people let their dreams deflate because of delays. When things are not happening fast enough, we tend to get discouraged. As you open you cell group, don't let go of your dream if your cell group is not growing as fast as you expected. Delays are not denials. Every dream has a future, no matter how long the delay. Keep on keeping on. Don't become inactive. For 1% of action is worth more than 100% intent. What you need to do is start your dream. Your dream does not begin until you start. Just do it. Burn every bridge of retreat to your past. Feed your faith. Slay all dream-killing words and starve your doubts. Cultivate your dreams. No dreams will flourish in the soil of doubt. If you doubt, you will do without. Declare today, "This day belongs to my dream." When you get up each morning, say to yourself, "This day belongs to my God-given vision."

Faith says, "This dream is going to happen." Faith reasons, "All things are possible with God." Speak words of faith to yourself. Remind yourself of all the possibilities God has for you. When God gives us a dream to reach the multitudes, he does it to stretch your faith. So flex your faith. Let your faith dream the big dreams. Are you sure about what God is sure about? Let your dreams be full of assurance. Don't let doubt creep in. When in doubt, people make the mistake of adjusting the promise, instead of the premise. Don't adjust the promise, adjust your attitude. Dreams have a faith mindset that says, "If God said it, that settles it."

People without dreams are people without purpose. And people without purpose are people with dreamless prayers. If you have no dreams, there will be no purposeful prayers in your life. The prayers that God listens to are those with purpose. God is not into meaningless prayers, as mentioned in Matthew 6:7. Meaningless prayers are impotent religious prayers. You will never change your present situation until your determine your future destination.

God uses men that consistently dream big dreams. Why? Nothing happens until someone starts dreaming. A real man or woman of God is someone who is not afraid to believe God. Dream big dreams, pray big dreams, speak big dreams, and envision big dreams, for dreaming is the language of the Holy Spirit. A man never outgrows his dream. Ask yourself, "What would I attempt for God if I knew I couldn't fail?" The Bible says in Ephesians 3:20, "God is able to do exceedingly above whatever we can ask or think." The problem with many church people today is that they set their dreams too low.

Some people do not catch the vision because all they pray is "Lord bless what I am doing," while they should be praying, "Help me to do what you are doing, take me to what you are already blessing." For some people, their dreams end up being a nightmare because they were not really of God.

When you have a dream from God, you will be willing to take risks. In Acts 15:26, we find, "They risked their lives for the name of our Lord Jesus Christ." The disciples were willing to risk it all to see the world come to Jesus. On the other hand, we find in Matthew 25 that the unfaithful servant is someone who is unwilling to take risks. What we need to learn is that where God guides He provides. Someone once said, "If you are not living on the edge, you are taking up too much space." Satan's greatest tool against people dreaming today is fear of failure. In Proverbs 29:25

we are told, "The fear of man brings a snare, but he who trusts in the Lord will be exalted." Amazingly, fear is actually a trap. God uses a man who expects to be used. The difference between winners and losers is whether you have a dreaming attitude. Never let an impossible situation intimidate you; instead, let it motivate you. Today's impossible problem is tomorrow's miracle. A man or woman with a dream is one who never gives up. Great dreamers are just ordinary people who don't give up. Did you know you are never a failure until you give up? There is one thing you do have control over, that is the choice on how much you will believe God for. Dreamers are determined to only to give up giving up. Choose to battle against discouragement today.

God says to you today, "How far you can see is how far I can bless you." It is a spiritual exercise to see what God sees. Your dream will determine your potential. Your dream from God will become your preferred future and destiny. Like Pastor Andy Stanley says, "Dreams and visions will become your clear mental picture of what it could be, fueled by the conviction that it should be." What you see, you seize. God has given you the title deed already, now go and possess the land. Abraham was pregnant with a dream and a vision, while Sarah was pregnant with Isaac. What are you pregnant with?

When you dream you live in the future. When we live in the future, all our past successes encourage us and our past failures become lessons to prepare us for the future. When you dream you gain focus. The power of a focused life will bring things into existence through the power of God beyond your imagination. Your life becomes like a spiritual magnifying glass that can set others on fire for God.

The Disciple Maker and His Family

God does not just want you to serve Him; He wants you and your family serving him together. His vision is to set up a priestly family in your household. You cannot rest until everyone in your family is serving God. You cannot be satisfied with just yourself in the vision.

If you have family members who are not serving the Lord, continue to love them. Your unbelieving family may doubt what you say, but they will always believe what you do. James chapters 2 and 3 instruct us that our faith is only believable to others when we put it into action. Our faith becomes incarnated and visible to your   family   when   you   live   it.

The vision and spiritual gifts

The Bible is very clear that disciples have been given spiritual gifts (Ephesians 4:10-13, 1 Corinthians 12-14, Romans 12:3-8). The gifts of the Spirit are an endowment of special grace to be able to do something you were not able to do before. Of course, these gifts are used to bless, edify, and strengthen the body of Christ. In some churches, each believer has a gift or gifts to do exclusive ministry through this empowerment. A believer may have the gift of healing and say, "I have the gift of healing and this is all I do," or "I have the gift of teaching and all I do is teach." Their main concern is the use of their gift that excludes them in to a particular ministry. But the Bible presents to us a higher perspective and point of view. What we find is that the gifts are given to each believer to make disciples. In the Old Testament the prophets had disciples. We find that Elijah discipled Elisha (2 Kings 2:1-13). We find that Moses discipled Joshua. The passing on of the gift (Numbers 11:11 and 25) occurs as a direct commission to shepherd the people of God. John the Baptist, the greatest Old Testament prophet who ever lived had disciples. His prophetic ministry was not separate from making disciples. I say all of this because there are people who want to use the gifts of the Spirit, but do not want to make disciples. We do not find this practiced in the Scriptures. In 1 Corinthians 1:26 it says, "What then is the outcome (of the use of the gifts of the Spirit), brethren? When you assemble, *each one* has a psalm, has a teaching, has a revelation, has a tongue, has an interpretation. Let all things be done for edification." You will never find a separation of the gifts with teaching and mentoring in the Bible. Why? It's because you will never have true lasting transformation without the impartation of a mentor and leader. In 1 Tim. 4:14, Paul exhorts Timothy, his protégé, to "stir up the gift that was given through the laying of hands of the leadership." Notice again, how discipleship and mentorship is never separated from the use of the gifts of the Spirit. There are people in churches who want to be teachers, apostles, pastors, and prophets, etc., but do not want to make disciples. They hide behind their titles and pulpits. They don't want to get their hands dirty and get involved in people's lives. Ministry is cleaning up other people's messes and restoring them in Christ. When Jesus wanted to explain what ministry was all about to the disciples in John 13, he pulled out a towel and began to clean up the dirt of the disciples' feet (v.5). Here we find the Master Teacher Jesus with a towel in his hands. If we separate people to operate solely using their gifts and separate them from their mandate to disciples, we will end up with a church of consumers because people will do what leaders do.

The gifts were often manifested in a small group setting (I Corinthians 14). The church met largely in cell groups and there they each used their gift to bless one another. The movement of the Holy Spirit in small home group gatherings seems to be the pattern in the Scriptures. When was it that the first disciples received the baptism with the Holy Spirit with the evidence of speaking of tongues? It was during a small home group gathering with Peter (Acts 10:1-48).

There are 29 gifts of the spirit mentioned in the Word of God (Romans 12; 1 Peter 4:10-11, 1 Corinthians 12). They all have different functions (Romans 12:4) but the same purpose (Matthew 28:18-19). Unto each believer has been given a different grace to minister to the body. What we find in the Scriptures is that you cannot separate the Great Commission from the power of God. The power of God was given to fulfill the purpose of God (Acts 1:8). The outpouring of gifts was directly related to the Great Commission.

In Ephesians 4:10-13, we find a list of the "five fold ministries." Though they are never mentioned by that name in this passage, many have attached this label to these five ministries. In the vision, we find the gifts and ministries demonstrated. When we win souls, we are doing the work of an evangelist (2 Timothy 4:5). When we consolidate and mentor, we do the work of a prophet (Mark 1:2-3). When we disciple, we are doing the work of a pastor and teacher (1 Thessalonians 5:12). When we send, we are doing the work of an apostle. The word apostle itself literally means "sent out one." This is why Jesus is called an apostle (Heb. 3:11). These five fold ministries are mentioned to show the church what they ought to do: win, consolidate, disciple and send. Ephesians 4:12 tells us that they were given unto people in the church for their "equipping." Leaders equip others to do the work necessary in the Body of Christ. There are people in the church who have an extraordinary gift to encourage others to do the work of God. Though the pastor may enjoy discipling people in the church, the evangelist encourages him to do the work of an evangelist by winning souls (2 Timothy 4:5). The apostle will equip others with a sending anointing. The prophet will impart a consolidating anointing. The evangelist will equip us with a winning anointing. And, the pastor or teacher will impart a discipling anointing upon us. This is true leadership. The biblical definition of leadership is placing yourself in service of others so they might become what God wants them to be. How do we know who has which particular gift? If you have the gift, it will show in your work. It is something that God has given you and becomes part of who you are. It will become your never-ending interest and passion. Paul puts it this way in 1 Corinthians 15:10: "By the grace of God I am what I am, and his grace toward me did not prove vain; but I labored even more than all of the others, yet not I, but the grace of God with me."

The work through the gifts is for construction, not destruction. It should bring the membership to unity (Ephesians 4:13). Each was given to bring the body together to love like Jesus. It should bring the membership to maturity (v. 13). Grow to look at and live like Jesus. It should bring the membership to ministry (v.12), to labor like Jesus. The aim of every gift of the Spirit is bring people to become like Jesus. When we are like Jesus, we will be healthy Christians. When you have healthy Christians, you will have a healthy church. When you have a healthy church, you will have healthy growth. How? We do this through "equipping" (some translations "perfecting") one another. The word "equip" means to put a thing into a condition in which it ought to be. We are to disciple one another to become what we ought to be: like Jesus.

How to have a quality ministry

A quality ministry does not happen by chance. In the book of 1 Corinthians we find the secrets to a five star ministry.

Servant attitude: Paul tells us in the first four chapters of 1 Corinthians that true ministry is serving one another. The secret in growing a quality ministry is to do it with an attitude of servanthood. Ministry is servanthood. So regardless what gift of the Spirit God will use through you, we are to do it in a spirit of a servant. There is no ministry without servanthood. We must love to serve and serve to love. You can't love without serving. The aim of every ministry is to serve. Since the heart of ministry is to serve, choose to serve well. Serve better than you would if you were working in a five star hotel. Why? Because, when we serve others, we are really serving the King of Kings.

At the close of Jesus' ministry, during the Last Supper, He walked into a room of disciples and smelled something funny among them. Keep in mind that Jesus had been with them for three and a half years. He had poured his life unto them. They were it! There was no plan B. What did He smell in that room? He smelled pride, arrogance, unhealthy competition, selfishness, and pride. Peter had a sword in his hand, Judas was ready to betray him, and others were competing to see who would sit next to Jesus once He established His throne. He smelled competition rather than cooperation. Jesus began to pray openly before the disciples (John 17). In this prayer He prayed five times that they may be "one." Unity is the statement that makes us credible to the world. This is

172

the only prayer of Jesus that still needs to be answered. Jesus prayed and raised the dead. But how is it that the church is still not one? It is because for God is easier to raise a dead body than to break through a self-centered disciple. If you learn to serve, Jesus will grant you access to places that you never imagined possible and were previously off limits to you. Unity can only be created by those who are willing to serve. The answer to division in church is servanthood. A quality ministry is one that is based on the foundation of serving one another. If you develop a ministry of serving one another, you will automatically grow a ministry that will experience oneness. And Jesus promised that when you reach this level of oneness, the "world will believe" (John 17:21). True spiritual authority is gained through servanthood. The disciples initially thought that it would be gained through a title or getting on the good side of Jesus (Luke 22:24-27). It was an issue that Jesus had ministered to them before, but they had not learned at that point (Mark 9:34-37). Greatness comes through serving one another.

If you can't serve those who you can see, how will serve Him who you can't see? The fact is that you serve God by serving others. To the degree you are serving others, you are serving God.

Pay the Price: Ministering to others is costly. Quality has value and whatever has value is costly. Ministry is work. Work is effort plus energy. Energy and effort are costly. Normally, the greater the quality and the greater the ministry, the more it going to cost you. But the more it cost you, the greater the quality your ministry will have. 1 Corinthians 3:13 tells us that what the Lord is looking for is quality in our ministry. Someone who is not willing to pay the price in ministry is just taking up space. The good news is that there is a reward for those who minister with quality (v.13).

Develop Skills: In 1 Corinthians 3:10, we are told to build a quality ministry skillfully. Exodus 35:35 indicates that the Lord "has filled them with skills." The word "skilled" in Hebrew means "wisdom of heart." Developing quality disciples is a supernatural process that requires divine skills and strategy. Proverbs 24:3 says that a "house is built by wisdom". Skills help you develop a quality ministry fast, effectively and efficiently. As a disciple maker and leader, take time to develop leadership and ministerial skills. Skills can be learned. We are not born with skills, they are simply learned. This is why leaders are learners. And if we stop learning we stop leading.

Build carefully: In 1 Corinthians 3:10, we are told, "each man must be careful how he builds on it." A quality ministry must be tailored to its own specifications. For example, a first class suit is tailored to fit just right. God want to use you to raise twelve people in your group, but each one will need specific attention. Each member will require special attention, since their needs and gifts are different.

Build with class: In 1 Corinthians 3:12, Paul mentions that we can build with different levels of quality. He mentions gold and silver as the highest quality ministry. Paul understood class. There is a vast difference between a Phantom Rolls Royce and a Pinto automobile. There is a difference in the elegance and excellence of it. As disciple makers, we must learn to walk and live in honor as mentioned in II Timothy 2:21, "Therefore, if any one cleanses himself from these things, he will be a vessel of honor, sanctified, useful to the Master, prepared for every good work." I want to challenge you to do ministry at a level that is useful to the Lord.

Attend to details: As stated before the difference between a five star hotel and a budget inn is attention to detail. We must pay attention to every aspect of the vision, not just the parts we like. A great architect pays attention to detail. And as a disciple maker, learn to pay attention to the details of how you present yourself, talk to others, show love, serve one another, and the way you love God.

You can count on it to last: A ministry build on quality will be consistent and it will not just be a spurt of charisma. Something with quality will not easily fade away. It is durable under pressure and stress.

Closing Thoughts

It is up to you to put to practice what you have learned in this book. It will change your life. If you do God's work God's way, you will end up with God's favor and fruit. The time is now. Your future is just one decision away. You will become a servant to whatever decision you make. Make up your mind today to give your life to the call of God. Yield to His beckoning call and change the world. There is nothing more exciting than to be used by God. Catch the fire of God and go and set the world on fire for God. God's got your back. He will be with you every step of the way. If not now, then when? If it is not you, who then will go? The time is now and you are the one. Run with the vision. Be who you already are – A Disciple Maker!